EASTERN ENCOUNTERS

MICHAEL WYNNE-PARKER

authorHOUSE

AuthorHouse™ UK
1663 Liberty Drive
Bloomington, IN 47403 USA
www.authorhouse.co.uk
Phone: UK TFN: 0800 0148641 (Toll Free inside the UK)
UK Local: (02) 0369 56322 (+44 20 3695 6322 from outside the UK)

© *2022 Michael Wynne-Parker. All rights reserved.*

No part of this book may be reproduced, stored in a retrieval system, or transmitted by any means without the written permission of the author.

Published by AuthorHouse 08/24/2022

ISBN: 978-1-7283-7466-6 (sc)
ISBN: 978-1-7283-7467-3 (hc)
ISBN: 978-1-7283-7465-9 (e)

Print information available on the last page.

Any people depicted in stock imagery provided by Getty Images are models, and such images are being used for illustrative purposes only. Certain stock imagery © *Getty Images.*

This book is printed on acid-free paper.

Because of the dynamic nature of the Internet, any web addresses or links contained in this book may have changed since publication and may no longer be valid. The views expressed in this work are solely those of the author and do not necessarily reflect the views of the publisher, and the publisher hereby disclaims any responsibility for them.

Other books by Michael Wynne-Parker

Bridge Over Troubled Water 1989

The Mandana Poems 1998

Reflections in Middle Years 2005

Wilson Lutara-A Man of Africa 2007

We Shall Fly 2009

If My Table Could Talk 2011

For Nicole Rose Fitzgerald

HISTORICAL PERSPECTIVE

969-978 Prince Vladimir Svyatoslavich of Novgorod Vladimir The Great, First sole Ruler of The Rus.

978 The conquest of Kiev which becomes the first capital of The Rus

988 Russia becomes Christian-
The Baptism of The Rus.

1108 City of Vladimir becomes the capital

1147-aproximately Moscow becomes the capital

1712 St.Petersburgh becomes the capital of The Russian Empire.

1918 Moscow becomes the capital of The Union of Soviet Socialist Republics-USSR

1991 Moscow is capital of The Russian Federation.

CONTENTS

Acknowledgements xiii
Preface xv
Introduction xix

1. Early Days 1

2. Tajikistan 5
   Dushanbe 5
   Probing the Depths 7
   Trajic Air 10

3. Russian Enterprise, Part 1 17
   Moscow/DSL Alpha 17

4. Russian Culture, Part 1 21
   Moscow 21
   Rostov-on-Don 24

5. Ukraine 25
   Russians and Ukrainians in London 25
   Kiev 27
   Crimea 31

6. Estonia 37
   The Two Estonias 37
   The Old Town 42
   Fire 47
   Magical Manors 54
   Pühtitsa 59
   Majesty 65
   Fragile Union 78

7. Russian Enterprise, Part 2 92
   Russian Railways 92
   The North Caucasus 98

8. Russian Culture, Part 2 110
   SAMBO 112
   Imperial Orthodox Palestine Society 121
   Russkiy Mir Foundation 128
   M.ART Foundation 131
   Ludvig Nobel Prize 133
   Orthodox Russia 136

9. Afterthought 156

ACKNOWLEDGEMENTS

I am grateful to all my friends within Russia, Ukraine, Estonia, and beyond who have inspired and contributed to this book. Friendship encircles the globe, and trust and loyalty are its essence.

Many friends and acquaintances have encouraged me to write as I speak, and in story form. You know who you are!

Special thanks to Emily Field, who has diligently deciphered my handwriting to produce the manuscript, and to my publisher for guiding the project through to completion.

PREFACE

PRINCESS GYTHA

The remarkable story of a slaughtered king's daughter who marries an early Kievan prince, becomes mother of twelve, and ancestor of the British monarchy!

Long ago, the daughter of the last English king suddenly left for Denmark. Her name was Princess Gytha, and her father, King Harold, whether by intelligence, intuition, or simply logic, knew he would die in the forthcoming Battle of Hastings. The year was 1066—in my day, a year remembered by every schoolboy—and the Normans were about to invade and conquer the ancient English kingdom.

Sure enough, the French won a decisive victory. King Harold was slain, and the Godwinson dynasty ended.

However, Princess Gytha, surely sad and homesick,

was safely in friendly Denmark and soon to embark on the journey of a lifetime—to Russia.

Russia, in those days, was known as the land of the Rus, and very little was known about it in the West. Over centuries, the huge country has slowly evolved, uniting a variety of ethnic groups from East and West, from Finland to Mongolia, and had just a few years before Gytha arrived embraced Christianity.

It happened like this. During the decline of the ancient Rus kingdom, the principality of Kiev emerged, known as the Kievan Rus. The first grand prince (or king) was Vladimir the Great. Aware of the discord caused by a multiplicity of religious factions, he sent emissaries abroad, commanding them to find the true religion if such existed. Some of them ended up in Constantinople, where they experienced the Orthodox liturgy in all its grandeur and beauty. They were convinced that this was indeed the true religion.

Returning to Prince Vladimir, they convinced him that what he had sought had been found, and Vladimir requested representatives of the new religion to visit Kiev. They so much inspired him that he was baptised, followed by the baptism of the majority of the people. This is known as the baptism of the Rus. The year is 988.

No one knows why Princess Gytha travelled to Russia, and there is little known about the circumstances in which she was introduced to Grand

Prince Vladimir's grandson, also Vladimir, known as Vladimir Monomach. It is probable that as the daughter of the recent king of England, she would meet the royal family of any country she visited.

Amazingly, soon after her arrival, Gytha and Vladimir married in the Cathedral of Our Saviour in Chernigov in 1074, just eight years after her father's death at the Battle of Hastings.

Little is known about Princess Gytha's life in Russia except that it was long, she died in 1107, and that she had twelve children! The eldest son, Mstislav the Great, became the last ruler of the united Kievan Rus. However, according to Russian historian Vladimir Medinsky, Gytha was a significant influence on her husband's public relations: "Knyaz's English wife wasn't wasted" (Medinsky quotes M. P. A. Kekseev's comparative analysis between Monomakh's writings and Alfred the Great's). Monomakh himself referred to her in his own book of instructions for his sons: "Love your wives, but grant them no power over you."

Gytha outlived her husband, and in the Patericon of St Pantaleon Cloister in Cologne it is recorded that "Gytha the Queen died as a nun."

Her legacy certainly lived on. Through her son Mstislav the Great, she is an ancestor of King Edward III of England, and hence of all subsequent English and British monarchs!

She has the distinction of being a direct ancestor

of St Alexander Nevsky, one of the greatest heroes of Russian history. More of him in a later chapter.

Of the many descendants of Gytha, I was fortunate to meet the Obolenskys. Firstly Serge, who demonstrated the dagger dance on the table of the Waldorf Astoria Hotel in New York, and lately, Selene Obolensky, the famous map expert in London. Both referred to their unbroken descent from Monomakh and Gytha.

Certainly King Harold would have been extremely proud of his daughter. She had clearly inherited his bravery and courage.

This amazing story sets the scene for the developing English-Russian cultural ties which have bound our two countries for a thousand years. Whilst politics divides, culture unites!

INTRODUCTION

Eleven years have passed since I last recorded the whispers of conversation heard around my table. Life has accelerated at a rapid pace leaving little time for writing recollections. However, suddenly, today Saturday 17th August 2019, I feel compelled to take up my pen and write.

After the exhilarating encounters with Vera Protosova referred to in the final chapter of 'If my Table Could Talk'[1], I made a momentous decision. I was to leave London and settle for the next twelve years in Tallinn.

Though it has been said that those who 'tire of London tire of life'[2], after twelve years of living there, without a country retreat of my own, I fled!

The final decision was made on a packed underground train, during rush hour, when a poor child vomited against my back, saturating my shirt and trousers. I

---

[1] If My Table Could Talk by Michael Wynne-Parker, first published by Authorhouse 2011.
[2] Dr Samuel Johnson 1709-1784.

rushed home, threw off the soiled clothes, and took a long cleansing shower.

As often in life a 'sign' had been given and I realised that packed trains, chaotic traffic, noise and increasing pollution were no longer for me.

I first visited Estonia on the prompting of Andrew Rosindel MP[3] who had invited me to address a conference in Tallinn on the subject of conservative values in contemporary society. Andrew had no idea the 'Pandora's Box' he was opening! And at the time, nor had I.

On the surface the UK MPs largely viewed Estonia as an independent state recently liberated from the Soviet Union. And indeed so it was. However underneath the facade lay a seething disharmony. I had to be there to begin to understand this and its vital implications that have become clear as time has passed.

Within a year of arriving in Tallinn I moved my residential base to a fourteenth century house in the Old Town.

Between 2002 and 2013 I spent most of my time in Tallinn with regular monthly visits to London.

As the digital age was dawning, I quickly realised that most business matters could be dealt with wherever one was actually based, once close ties had been established, and that one no longer needed to live in an aeroplane.

---

[3] Chapter 5 'Estonia'

Hence my Introcom[4] activities developed in the Middle East, Europe and Russia continued to flourish. In addition, I wrote three books which would not have been possible in the frantic life of London. My residential time in Tallinn ended in 2013 and now I dwell in the peace and tranquillity of rural Norfolk again.

Frequent visits to London convince me that rural life is best. The digital age seems now almost out of control and mobile devices have become dangerous addictions.

I am writing this on my terrace looking across to the garden, now organic, pulsating with life and the increasing habitat of bees, butterflies and songbirds.

Thankfully this estate has been in the same family for over two hundred years[5]. There is a rhythm to daily life. People know and respect each other - there is cultural identity and harmony.

But sadly this is increasingly rare in the UK. Tony Blair's[6] multiculturalism and subsequent government's obsession with political correctness are really gaining ground in all metropolitan areas and will likely finally destroy the intrinsic fabric of this realm.

The politicians are simply pawns in a bigger game,

---

[4] Introcom International Ltd.
[5] This was written whilst I was living in Woodbastwick, Norfolk. The estate has been in the Cator family for over 200 years.
[6] Sir Anthony Charles Lynton Blair KC. Prime Minister of the UK, 1997-2007.

American led consumerism swamps the markets where old is out and new is essential.

The shopping mall has replaced the church in the UK and the historic Judaic Christian heritage is in tatters.

All this has happened in an alarmingly short time. Living in Tallinn for those 11 years only emphasised to me the dramatic change going on in the UK.

Living in Estonia with its close proximity to Russia showed me how years of atheistic communism had resulted in an instinctive desire to get back asap to 'roots.' For Estonians a desire for national identity. For Russians a desire for their Byzantine heritage.

Their two desires are not as incompatible as they may seem.

All our roots are in the soil. Once rooted we have a natural appreciation of creation and all its significance and beauty. Dostoyevsky[7] showed us how this beauty is the face of God. This fulfilment is not attained by political correctness, consumerism, or 'rights', but by connection with our roots and living responsibly.

Without identity a human develops 'dis-ease'. Thus multiculturalism is the opposite of harmony. Every child born of two parents - male and female - gains natural identity which quickly extends into the wider family and the family into the community. Traditional

---

[7] Fyoder Dostoyevsky 1821-1881

family values are formed therefore which is why they are generally disparaged by the liberal elite who dominate politics and the media today.

Thankfully there are still noble souls who dispense wisdom and human kindness. As revealed in my last volume 'If My Table Could Talk' I have been most fortunate to meet some of these exceptional people. This volume continues to introduce the reader to those who have graced my life in the Russia, Ukraine, and Estonia.

1

EARLY DAYS

I am often asked what influenced me to visit Russia.

My father had some books about Russia which I inherited. They were written in the time of the Soviet Union, a rather different place from either ancient Russia or the Russia of today.

Very early in my life I encountered Russian Orthodoxy and, rather like Grand Prince Vladimir, felt it was the true religion! Or at least the highest form of ancient Christianity present in the modern world.

I met Russians who had fled the Soviet Union and their children who were brought up in the West—London, Paris, or New York. I devoured every book of nineteenth- and twentieth-century Russian history and enjoyed discussing them with my new Russian friends.

But my first actual encounter with Russia came in an entirely different way.

Visualise a hotel bar in Helsinki in 1990. The Finns knew how to drink, and the bar was noisy and full of cigarette smoke. Ordering a large vodka, I bumped into an impressive figure of military bearing and jovial manner. A few drinks later, and with a quickly established mutual understanding, I was shocked to be told that the Soviet Union was shortly to collapse into chaos as a direct result of the Afghan war.

No invader has ever conquered Afghanistan, as indeed the United States recently discovered. More profoundly, *all* empires end with military expansion resulting in deadly economic cost.

My mysterious friend informed me in that Helsinki bar exactly what would happen one year later—on 26 December 1991—the end of the Soviet Empire.

Soon after this chance encounter, I met Alexi Safarov. Alexi was born in Dushanbe, Tajikistan, and was well acquainted with the Soviet leadership and confirmed what I learned in the bar was true. Tajikistan borders with Afghanistan, and Alexi was fully aware of the perilous situation.

Then he challenged me: "Are you prepared to take advantage of the opportunities that will present themselves in the midst of the forthcoming transition?"

It was this challenge that led me to investigate what practical areas of lucrative business would probably open. An obvious one to be considered was security.

Enter Frank Noah, Richard Bethel (now Lord

Westbury[8]), and Alastair Morrison. Frank was an established banker, and together Richard and Alastair had founded DSL Holding Limited, then a member of the Hambro International Banking and Financial Services Group.

I had met Richard Bethel through his father[9] in northern Cyprus in 1990. He had a distinguished career in the Special Air Services (SAS) and Scots Guards, where he earned the nickname Tarzan, and a natural flair for business.

Alastair Morrison, also SAS, became famous for his role in the successful rescue of hostages held in an aeroplane in Mogadishu, Somalia, in 1977.

SAS soldiers are well known for their courage in the face of every danger, and thus DSL appeared to be the perfect group to embark on a Russian adventure.

Before relating what happened next, I must introduce another personality who was to play centre stage in a far-flung part of the disintegrating Soviet Union.

Enter Peter Barnes-Graham, who together with Richard Wilkins, started the Tajik Development Agency in early 1991.

In August that year, Peter, invited me to a meeting to discuss my interest in Russia and the possibility of mutual commercial cooperation. Clearly their main

---

[8] Richard Nicholas Bethel, sixth Baron Westbury.
[9] David Allan Bethel, fifth Baron of Westbury.

focus was on generating business with Tajikistan, and up popped the name Alexi Safarov!

From the beginning there was an element of mystery surrounding Alexi. However, he proved to be a reliable friend and business partner both in our dealings with DSL(more later) and in Tajikistan, providing introductions at the highest level.

2

TAJIKISTAN

Dushanbe

On 6 October 1991, during John Major's premiership, I was joined by Alexi, Peter Barnes-Graham, and Richard Wilkins on my first exciting visit to Dushanbe, the capital of Tajikistan. The flight from Moscow was memorable. A plane had been chartered, and we climbed aboard only to find a long table loaded with food and bottles around which we sat. A man in uniform sat down on my right, knocked back a large vodka, and announced that he was our pilot. No health and safety in those days!

Despite the booze, the flight was smooth, and we arrived safely in Dushanbe in a rather jolly and very excited mood.

Tajikistan is surrounded by rugged mountains with snow-capped peaks rising over 5,000 metres (16,400 feet). Dushanbe made a good first impression with wide boulevards lined with trees and surrounded by parks and flower-filled gardens.

The Tajik people only came under Russian rule in the 1860s. Following the Russian Revolution, they were absorbed into the Soviet sphere.

From the sight of the first mosque, the atmosphere felt more Middle Eastern than Russian, though the Soviet influence was still evident. The name Dushanbe should have been the obvious first clue as to the dominant culture for it means "Monday" in Persian.

Yes, we quickly discovered the historic Iranian heritage and that the form of Islam here was distinctly Shia, rather than the more strait-laced Sunni tradition.

I well remember our early invitation to lunch by the chief imam after an interesting visit to the principal mosque. It was a surprise and rather a relief when he produced a bottle of excellent local wine.

Many interesting exploratory meetings took place over the next few days with politicians, businessmen, and other notables. There was a visit to the newly formed bank in which I opened an account literally on the back of an envelope. I realised I would probably never see that deposit again.

Memorable also was a dinner held in the first minister's dacha. Apart from ourselves were the head of the newly independent army, governor of the central bank, and the first minister. I well understood what the form would be: innumerable toasts in Russian style. Thus the speeches and toasts began over the next couple of hours. Deciding I would have to prove that an Englishman never gets drunk at the table, I was able to discreetly pour most of my vodka into a conveniently placed large bowl of flowers. By the time my turn came to speak and lift my glass, the evening was extremely jolly, and luckily so, as at that moment the flowers in front of me flopped dramatically on the table, having absorbed about a litre of alcohol. As we rose, the first minister was about to say, "Amazing, you Englishmen outdrink us all." I am not sure whether my reputation was enhanced or diminished!

Nothing practical actually immediately resulted from this first visit, though it was to lead to two projects in due course, for better or worse!

Probing the Depths

A few weeks after the first visit to Dushanbe, Alexi called me with an interesting story.

It is known that during the Soviet period, scientific developments were well advanced; some suspected far in advance of those in the West. Without realising it, we had witnessed one such development during the visit. It seemed like any other laboratory to inexperienced eyes and left little impression. However, what Alexi had to say made more than just an impression; it led to an adventure!

The name of the laboratory is unpronounceable, but here it is: Tajikaerocosmogeodesia. It transpired that the scientists had developed a method of precisely locating the presence of oil or gas in the depths of the earth. The original technique had been created in Germany and refined by scientists Ishanov and Pilgovi, and it had become a closely guarded secret. Alexi explained that all I needed to know was that the methodology combined satellite photos with a secret drilling technique.

The challenge for me was to find a country known to have oil and gas that had not yet been exactly located. For many years, I had been involved in several Middle Eastern countries, and this seemed to be the obvious area to begin my research. However, a few days after Alexi's call, I happened to be lunching with Bernard Schreier,[10] a prominent businessman with strong Israeli connections. Bernard was fully aware of my strong support for the Palestinians, but as usual, business always puts political opinion into perspective!

Bernard was fascinated to hear of the amazing Tajik technology. Together with our legal adviser, John Beveridge QC, we set about a plan to get the scientists with the equipment firstly to London and then secretly into Israel. It was no mean feat to get the scientists and their associates from Dushanbe to London, challenged by visa requirements and language barriers. Because

---

[10] Sir Bernard Schreier, 1921–2013.

of their secret knowledge, they had been virtually prisoners in their laboratory, so to venture forth for the first time on a plane to London was in itself an adventure. And once they encountered the sights of London, we wondered whether they would ever wish to return home.

After a couple of days clarifying all arrangements, including their first ever commercial contract, we were ready to embark for Tel Aviv. I say *we* as it was agreed that it was essential that I accompany them. This meant urgently getting a new passport as mine was full of Arab visas which would not go down well in Tel Aviv.

Finally, all was ready, and I made my one and only journey into a country incognito.

On arrival, we were swiftly taken to a secret location. It was actually a pleasant, small hotel on the seashore, where I was to remain more or less confined for the next few days.

The scientists set off each morning after breakfast to the location where it was known that oil and gas lay below the surface. After dinner each evening, the scientists reported their day with mesmerising enthusiasm as their secret analysis appeared to be getting them very close to an exact location.

A week later, their investigation completed, we quietly returned to London, and the scientists went back to their laboratory in Dushanbe to analyse their findings.

It was not long before I received the call. Yes, the oil was there, exactly at the place they located. But unfortunately, it was nearly two miles below the surface!

They say nothing ventured, nothing gained, and at the very least, this adventure was an amazing experience. Looking back, I wonder why we did not take the scientists to other oil-producing countries. But it was not to be, and I never saw or heard of them again.

Trajic Air

The second project discussed during my first visit to Dushanbe was the possible development of a Tajik international airline.

The idea was not entirely new to me. In London, before my departure, I had met with Bahman Daneshmand, an old friend of Asil Nadir[11] and aviation expert. He saw the enormous potential of opening routes between London and central Asia.

In April 1993, Deputy PM Samadov, whom I had last met at the memorable dinner in the Dacha, arrived in London to discuss the airline project about which he was passionate. He really wanted his own airline!

How would this operation be viable and profitable? In aviation terms, to operate between Dushanbe and London, rights under the sixth Freedom of the Air

---

[11] Asil Nadir, born 1941.

were required. The Freedoms of the Air, established in 1944, are a set of commercial aviation rights granting a country's airline the privilege of entering and landing in another country's airspace. In the case of Tajik Air, for this was to be the official name of the carrier, the third and fourth freedoms applied. These rights are agreed to between the home country and the other country in the form of an air services agreement. By using third and fourth agreement rights, a sixth freedom operation can be created, similar to a hub operation, with the home country being in the middle of the operation between two countries.

For Tajik Air to be viable, it was decided that the perfect route would be London Dushanbe, Delhi, and Karachi due to large numbers of Indians and Pakistanis living in the United Kingdom. By operating this schedule, it was felt that all the seats would be filled in a highly competitive market by offering good service with low fares. To deal with all the red tape in record time, Samadov instructed his foreign minister to appoint me as Tajik honorary consul with immediate effect. I was thus able to march into the Foreign and Commonwealth (F&C) Office to see my good friend Lord Caithness,[12] who was then minister of state for foreign and commonwealth affairs. We spent just an hour together, and the protocols were agreed on and

---

[12] Malcolm Ian Sinclair, twentieth Earl of Caithness.

signed. Surely an international record! In fact, what normally takes many months was achieved in just three weeks, and the actual arrangements for the airline could begin.

From the beginning, Margaret Thatcher[13] had been an enthusiastic supporter of our venture and used her influence to gain us a slot at Heathrow. Another remarkable feat for a start-up airline.

---

[13] Margaret Hilder Thatcher, 1925–2013, Baroness Thatcher, UK prime minister, 1979–1990.

MARGARET, THE LADY THATCHER, O.M., P.C., F.R.S.

HOUSE OF LORDS

LONDON SW1A 0PW

6th October 1993

Dear Mr. Wynne-Parker,

Thank you for your letter of 4th October. I was delighted to hear the good news about the joint Tajik Air enterprise. I think congratulations should be primarily bestowed on you.

Sadly, I cannot be with you on 11th October at the Carlton Club due to a prior engagement that evening. However, please pass on my very best wishes to everyone for an enjoyable evening.

With best wishes,

Yours sincerely

Margaret Thatcher

Mr Michael Wynne-Parker
Managing Director, INTROCOM Ltd

Between Samadov's visit in April and the ultimate launch of *Snow Leopard*—for this became the name of the Boeing 747SP leased from United Airlines—there was a flurry of activity.

An office was set up in Kensington High St, London. From there, ticket sales coordination with travel agents (this was before online booking), recruitment of the crew, and all other technical procedures would take place, all under the watchful eye of Bahman Danshmand.

Very important, of course, was the funding of the airline. This was accomplished through a UK company, of which the shareholders were the Tajik government and our London team on a fifty-fifty basis. It was agreed that the Tajiks would put up £2m, and we would be in charge of setting up and running the airline free of charge until it became profitable.

By 11 October 1993, everything was well underway, and an inaugural dinner was held for a hundred guests at the Carlton Club. We were all supremely confident in the success of our venture. Especially so as ticket sales were going extremely well.

Finally, at the end of November, the plane arrived at Stansted Airport, where it was rapidly hand-painted in the Tajik national colours. *Snow Leopard* was born!

How did we keep our nerves in those frantic days? I do not know!

After several delays, causing a huge headache for the travel agents—not to mention the passengers—the inaugural flight took place on 3 December 1993, two years after my first visit to Tajikistan. That inaugural flight was memorable. No aeroplane with the Boeing's wingspan had ever flown into Dushanbe before. The approach was through a mountain range. It seemed that the wings almost scraped the edge of the mountains, much to the consternation of the passengers. With a general sigh of relief, we landed, but then only to experience an extremely bumpy runway which resulted in the bursting of most of our tyres!

The final straw was the sight of a struggling goat being dragged across the tarmac towards the plane. In a ritual gesture, its throat was cut, splattering the plane steps with blood to the horror of passengers and crew alike.

Over the next few weeks, our flights took off at 11 p.m. from Heathrow, and all went smoothly—despite the pilot reporting a UFO—on all sixteen successful flights.

However, pressure began to mount as the weeks went by and no £2m had come from the Tajiks. As though to give us comfort, Samadov announced he would arrive in London on *his* plane. And amazingly, PM Thatcher decided to join us for dinner to welcome him. It was an interesting evening and should have set the stage for undoubted success as Samadov assured us that the money would arrive in the next few days.

It did not come.

Rumours abounded, including one that Samadov had transferred the cash to his personal account in Vienna.

John Beveridge QC warned us that to continue flights would risk the company trading insolvently, and that we British directors would be responsible!

Thus, most reluctantly, it was decided to cancel the next flight out of London. Lord Moyne, one of our directors, was given the unpleasant task of going to Heathrow to inform the four hundred passengers that there would be no flight. This began the fearful drama of the collapse of Tajik-Air, by now Trajic Air indeed!

As an afterthought, perhaps we were a little naive to expect a now tiny, fragile state to be able to perform responsibly, especially after so many years of communist rule. However, despite the sad consequences for passengers, crew, employees, and not least the hopeful directors, we had made aviation history as the first superjet ever to fly into Tajikistan.

1. The Hon. Desmond Guiness and Lord Moyne, Kadriorg Palace, Tallinn 2007.

3

RUSSIAN ENTERPRISE, PART 1

Moscow/DSL Alpha

Throughout my experiences in Tajikistan, my guide and mentor had been Alexi Safarov. Like all of us, he had been extremely disappointed by our two failed Tajik ventures, especially so as Tajikistan was his homeland.

However, dear reader, as gently hinted at in previous pages, Alexi was a man of many connections and especially so in Moscow—and at a high level. And it was to be through Alexi's introduction that the highly successful venture of DSL Alpha was born.

I have already introduced the leading lights of DSL UK, Richard Bethel and Alastair Morrison. And very soon, Alexi introduced us to our first Russian partner, Col. Mikhail Golovatov.

Col. Golovatov was the commander of the KGB military unit known as Alpha Group, or Spetsnaz, until 1992. It seemed amazing that DSL made up of

UK special forces personnel should link up with their Russian counterparts. Both had courage and daring in common with distinguished records of bravery. And both clearly had excellent business instincts.

With the demise of the Soviet Union, Alpha became a major Russian security firm known as Alpha B and was only too ready to join forces with DSL to create the first UK-Russian joint venture in the heady year of 1992.

Only a few months before, in December 1991, was the Russian Federation born. Or the old Russia reappeared after seventy-three years of Soviet rule.

To be in Moscow in those early years was stressful and exciting. Stressful to observe the somewhat chaotic conditions resulting from the sudden and largely unexpected transition from total state control to general lack of any control. Exciting to observe the enthusiasm of those we were privileged to meet and work with to grasp every available opportunity. We did not know that the next seven years would descend into general political, social, and commercial chaos, until December 1999, when Russia would really take off under President Putin.

It is very convenient for Western politicians to forget what an enormous transformation the Putin presidency has had on Russia. A blind eye was turned to the gold-rush environment, extreme corruption, and oligarchical theft dominating the scene whilst the US-led West

Eastern Encounters

endeavoured to exert control through World Bank loans, NGOs, and junk food! Much of Western hostility towards President Putin may conceal a shred of envy at his remarkable achievements, consistent popularity in the opinion polls, and the increasing feeling of stability amongst the general populace. One woman tellingly answered a Western journalist's question, "What about democracy?" with, "We prefer stability."

It was understandable that one of President Putin's top priorities was to completely pay off the World Bank loans as a testimony to Russia's independence.

However, despite the chaos of 1991, DSL Alpha got off to an amazing start. Alpha had inherited a large office in central Moscow from which Mikhail Golovatov ran his professional team, quickly adapting to commercial priorities. When starting up in a foreign country, success is based on an intimate knowledge of cultural complexities, as well as having access to local and national decision makers. Alpha brought this essential local experience and knowledge, while DSL contributed its unique experience of crisis management, threat assessment, and specialist manpower, together making a powerful cocktail.

Many opportunities presented themselves, and the team was well prepared to act for major Western companies entering the new Russian market. The first important breakthrough was a contract signed with Chevron Oil in July 1993 which became a major player throughout the Russian Federation to this day, with a turnover of billions of dollars.

The DSL Alpha venture proved to be a huge success story, contributing much to Russia's internal security arrangements as well as being highly profitable for all concerned.

Col. Golovatov sold his shares when the project ended for an estimated $200,000 million. He continues to preside over his business empire whilst enjoying his own equestrian farm.

Richard Bethel and Alastair Morrison sold their stakes in DSL very profitably and parted ways, setting up rival companies that eventually cashed in on the Iraqi reconstruction bonanza.

Alexi Safarov, though greatly disappointed in the failed Tajik ventures, could take great satisfaction in his introduction to Mikhail Golovatov and the amazing success story of DSL/Alpha.

4

RUSSIAN CULTURE, PART 1

Moscow

No one with the slightest knowledge of Russia can fail to be impressed by its cultural wealth, especially its literature and music. The obvious greats are Pushkin, Dostoyevsky, and Tolstoy. But close to them in my opinion is Bulgakov, especially his mysterious work, *The Master and the Margarita*.

I had struggled to read and understand this book for many years, so I was delighted when one day in December 2002, Vera Protosova[14] devoted an afternoon of discussion about it, culminating in a visit to Patriarch Ponds and to his Moscow apartment 50, at 10 Bolshaya Sadovaya.

Sitting on a bench—Was it the very one where the opening chapter begins?—it was very easy to imagine the book's unfolding dramatic events. And afterwards, climbing the staircase into the haunted atmosphere of the

---
[14] See final chapter of *If My Table Could Talk*.

apartment, one began to appreciate the significance of the book that Stalin had banned but only until his death.

We returned from the visit to read the book once again, but this time with a clearer understanding.

Above: 2. Patriarch Ponds, the setting for Bulgakov's *The Master and the Margarita*, Moscow 2002.

Right: 3. At Bulgakov's apartment, Moscow 2002.

With Vera I attended several magnificent operas at the Bolshoi. The first was memorable not only because of the performance but because of an encounter with two policemen as we walked to the car. "Passport please!" Unfortunately, I did not have mine with me. "Some questions then." It was freezing cold, so I suggested stepping inside a nearby restaurant. "So you don't like our weather." At this moment I found in my pocket a card both in Russian and English given to me by my friend Col. Mikhail Golovatov. Handing it to the police resulted in an immediate apology, "Excuse us please", and they departed. In 2002, police corruption was not uncommon, and Vera said I had a very lucky escape. Thankfully, in today's Russia, this would be much less likely to happen.

Michael Wynne-Parker

Rostov-on-Don

One of the earliest books I read on a Russian theme was *And Quiet Flows the Don*, by Mikhail Sholokhov. It was, therefore, with great excitement that I visited Rostov-on-Don in 2005. The book had been recommended to me by Count Nikolai Tolstoy, who first introduced me to the mythology and tradition of the Cossacks.

The Cossacks originated centuries ago, emerging along the banks of the rivers Dnieper, Don, and Terek, as well as the Ural river basins and famously in Zaporizhia (from whence came several characters in this book, Polina Volinsky, Julia Belokurova, and Edward Shyfrin). They evolved into democratic, self-governing, semi-military communities and played an important role in the historical and cultural development of Russia. The Soviets disbanded the Cossack units in the Soviet army, but in recent years, their descendants have revived their traditions and participation in national life. One of their strongest supporters is my good friend Nikolai Tolstoy.

It was a brief visit, allowing just time enough during a busy work schedule to stroll along the picturesque Don embankment, enjoying the green parks and lovely architecture.

I was reminded of this when recently talking at length to Natalia Lita, who elaborated on the Don Cossack tradition, somewhat amazed that I had actually read all three volumes of the famous book.

5

UKRAINE

Russians and Ukrainians in London

During the hectic 1990s, a great number of Russians began to arrive in London. Some I had first met in Moscow and was able to help them adjust to their new lives. Others I met for the first time in London. I will mention just three who made great impressions, not just because of their personality, but by the way they integrated into a very different environment.

First I met Polina Volinsky. Polina had arrived with her friends from Zaporizhia, the land of the Cossacks, in the new country of Ukraine. Her father had been a successful businessman until falling afoul of disreputable people who left him in severe financial difficulty, that sadly led to his premature death. Polina had invested in a small house in South London and set about developing her own business interests with a determination which was bound to lead to her ultimate success. Despite the harsh beginning in her newly adopted country, she is today a highly successful property developer, happily married with three children.

One evening Polina persuaded me to join her at an art exhibition. She told me that one of the organisers was a formidable woman, and thus I met Irina Emtseva. There was such a crowd at the gallery that I only managed a few words with Irina, but that was enough to leave a lasting positive impression. Irina went on to become one of the leading art dealers in London, specialising in bringing over from Russia talented young artists, thus enhancing the cultural life of the capital.

One day Polina brought her friend Julia Belokurova, also from Zaporizhia, to my London office, and we became immediate friends. Julia also struggled to find her role in London until finally finding her perfect position with the newly emerging *New Style* magazine. *New Style* went on to become today's leading Russian-British cultural, social, and fashion magazine with a growing international readership.

On my birthday in 2001, Julia accompanied me to a party thrown by Lady Olga Maitland at the Army Navy Club. Present was HRH Prince Michael of Kent, who is fluent in Russian and was delighted to engage in a long conversation with Julia in her native language. Assisted by a good flow of vodka, Julia enthused about her homeland, Ukraine, and to her surprise, the prince admitted that it was one part of the Russian sphere he had never visited.

At once Julia proclaimed, "Well, not to worry. Michael will arrange a visit!" The next day I received a call from Nicholas Chance, then head of the prince's office, thanking me for my kind offer and suggesting a date to meet and discuss arrangements. There was no escape!

Kiev

In the mid-nineties I had met Edward Shyfrin, amazingly also from Zaporizhia. Edward's story is as follows.

He had worked his way up from the shop floor to senior management in the Zaporizhian steel factory whilst also marrying his beautiful wife, Olga, and bringing up their children. They lived in a flat typical of the Soviet Union, with two rooms and basic shared facilities along the corridor.

When I met Edward, he had become a multimillionaire! As the Soviet Union crumbled, everything was for sale, including the steel factory. Edward's brother had escaped Zaporizhia a few years earlier and developed a successful business in Canada. Edward called him and asked him to send the few thousand dollars required to gain control of the factory. Thus, the previously hard-pressed worker became the energetic owner of the local steel business. And soon, he was the owner of the entire Ukrainian steel sector based in Kiev.

When I got to know Edward, he often looked rather withdrawn. One day I asked him why. "You will never understand," he said. "I was born in poverty and suddenly became a very rich man—a huge psychological shock to the system." I came across others like him, who somehow found it both hard to believe their luck and difficult to come to terms with all the responsibility of recently acquired vast wealth. It is interesting that many who win the National Lottery and find millions in their bank accounts seek counselling.

Edward, as with many Russians, has a sensitive nature and generous spirit. He and his wife were quickly drawn into philanthropic activities in London. I had the privilege of introducing them to Prince Michael of Kent who, as patron of Harefield Hospital, suggested Edward and Olga might like to support the appeal to extend the hospital's already famous premises. The hospital's main claim to fame was resident surgeon Dr Magdi Yacoub, who had become internationally acclaimed because of his pioneering work repairing heart valves and saving numerous lives.

During lunch I asked Dr Yacoub what his main advice was for middle-aged men. He replied take a 75mg dispersible aspirin daily. I have been doing this ever since, despite changing fashions in medical opinion. As I write, Sir Magdi Yacoub is still fighting fit at eighty-six.

Having already introduced Edward to Prince Michael, he was obviously the best person to consult about a visit to Kiev, that he agreed immediately to do.

Over the next few months, plans for the visit went ahead very smoothly, and the date was fixed. However, a few days before the planned departure from London, HM Queen Elizabeth, the Queen Mother, died on Saturday, 30 March. Of course, the visit was postponed until after the funeral, held on 9 April. So it was not until 10 April 2002 that HRH Prince Michael, Nicholas Chance, and myself got out from Heathrow to Kiev.

Edward Shyfrin had done a magnificent job in preparing the trip. On the first night, we were entertained to dinner by then president Kutchma's daughter, Olena, and her billionaire husband, Victor Pinchuk. Such was the success of the evening that the president not only extended the next day's original ten-minute royal audience to one hour but also put at our disposal his presidential jet for our forthcoming visit to Crimea.

Olena and Victor were newlyweds, and love was in the air. They took us the next day to visit the headquarters of the National Fund of Social Protection of Mothers and Children, introducing us to first lady Ludmilla Kuchma, its president. She was very gracious, warmly welcoming Prince Michael, who made a splendid speech enhanced by his Russian language skills.

The following day, we had two memorable meetings. In the morning, we visited the chief rabbi of Kiev, Yaakov Dov Bleich, a friend of Edward's who is Jewish, had funded the restoration of the central synagogue. Millions of Jews had been murdered in Soviet times, and Prince Michael felt strongly that we should pay appropriate tribute by visiting both the synagogue and Chief Rabbi Dov.

Diplomacy being at the heart of modern monarchy, we next visited the Metropolitan Vladimir, then head of the Russian Orthodox Church in Ukraine, who served us champagne and chocolates in a most convivial atmosphere.

No visit to Kiev would be complete without a visit to the Kiev Pechersk Laura, known as Monastery of the Caves, the first and most ancient monastery in Ukraine. It was founded in the mid-eleventh century by venerable St Anthony and St Theodosing of the caves. It contains the incorruptible relics of more than 120 saints.

The caves seem to go on forever, and we only managed to see a small part. There were tiny claustrophobic passages with the saints lying coffin to coffin on each side. The atmosphere is strange, mysterious, and dramatic at the same time. One cannot fail to be moved.

Crimea

On Saturday, 13 April, we boarded the presidential jet for the long-awaited visit to Crimea with bated breath and great expectations. We were not disappointed.

All the world seems to have been woven into the fabric of evolving Crimea—part of the Roman Empire, the Byzantium—settled by Seythians, Tauri, Greeks, Gorks, Huns, Bulgars, Kipchaks, and Khajars until becoming part of the Kievan Rus. Then came the Mongol invasions, part of the Golden Horde, followed by the Crimea Khanate and Ottoman Empire which was ultimately defeated by Catherine the Great in 1774. Perceptive visitors to Crimea today can perceive the influences of both Christian and Muslim heritages in the splendid architecture, amazingly preserved over the centuries.

In just three days, we got a taste of the magical atmosphere of Crimea and understood why Russians have made it a favourite holiday destination over the last hundred years or so.

It was a first visit for all of us and a great privilege for me to accompany Prince Michael to the places frequented and so loved by his relatives the late Tsar Nicholas and Empress Alexandra. He bears a striking resemblance to Tsar Nicholas, and many times, especially in churches, we saw people looking at him and likely wondering, *Has he returned?*

We arrived at Simferopol airport to be received by local dignitaries. Prince Michael was presented with the traditional bread and salt offered by attractive young women dressed in their distinctive national costumes. In Russia, bread is associated with hospitality and salt with long friendships. This truly set the scene for our memorable visit.

Outstanding memories are these.

Firstly, and to me the most memorable, was Livadia Palace, No one familiar with the last ruling Romanovs can fail to understand the love they had for Livadia. It represented tranquillity during increasingly turbulent times and a true and refreshing escape from onerous royal duties. To be there for the first time was truly moving, and I guess perhaps one of the highlights of Prince Michael's life. The curator was, of course, also amazed to be in the royal presence and surprised Prince Michael by presenting him—I think spontaneously—with an album of original Romanov photos. I thought of Nicholas and Alexandra as we strolled through the palace gardens, realising that only here could they walk freely and alone in complete safety.

Memorable was entering the room where Churchill,[15] Stalin,[16] and Roosevelt[17] met to sign the controversial Yalta Agreement in February 1945. If only one had

---

[15] Winston Leonard Spencer Churchill, 1874–1955.
[16] Joseph Vissarianovich Stalin, d. 1953.
[17] Franklin Delano Roosevelt, 1882–1945.

been a fly on the wall as these mighty men carved up and set the parameters of post-war Europe!

4. HRH Prince Michael of Kent examining photographs of the Russian imperial family, Livadia Palace, 2002.

5. In the Yalta Conference room. Note the British, US, and Soviet flags. Livadia Palace, 2002.

Again, Tsar Nicholas came into my mind as we entered the portals of the Massandra Winery. It is said his favourite tipple was Tokaji, normally associated with Hungary, and that Massandra had the best of its kind in Russia.

This famous winery was founded by Prince Lev Goltisyn in 1894 under the aegis of the tsar. Luckily, the huge collection of wines was hastily dispersed before the German occupation during the Second World War, but tragically, the winery's guest books disappeared too. Prince Michael, Nicholas Chance, and I were greeted by Sergei Foster, who had an interest in the winery and had kindly arranged and supervised our visit. It was memorable, indeed, except that we had difficulty in remembering leaving!

We enjoyed an amazing tour of the seemingly endless cellars containing innumerable bottles from floor to ceiling. Some were dated back to the late eighteenth century. One was dated 1775!

Though the historic guest books disappeared, we noticed several wall plaques dedicated to some of the famous visitors of the past—Chekhov, Gorky, Ho Chi Minh, and Tito.

After walking past over a million bottles, we were invited to sit in the directors' book room—at a table groaning with Russian salads, bread, and caviar—for a wine tasting. Good company, some of the finest wines, and a slowly evolving oblivion. I just remember we were all given dusty bottles of Tokaji labelled with the year of our births!

Vorontsov Palace is situated at the foot of the Crimean Mountains, near the town of Alupka. It is one of the most popular tourist attractions not to be missed. One of my favourite Russian writers is Ivan Bunin, and I first heard of the Vorontsov Palace in his poem 'Long Alley Leading Down to the Shore'. It aptly described the atmosphere of this amazing place.

The Vorontsov family played a leading role in Russian history over two centuries. Two aspects of the palace greatly impressed our party: the Islamic gardens contrasting with the English Tudor architecture. As we previously observed, Islam and Christianity both made important impacts on Crimean culture.

Sadly, we had only a couple hours to absorb the atmosphere of this remarkable place. We left feeling there was much more to see.

For Prince Michael, no visit to Crimea would have been complete without Balaclava, where the most decisive battle of the Crimean War was fought. The battle lasted just twenty minutes but was a totally unexpected disaster for the British and a remarkable victory for the Russians. We viewed the valley below us, and it took little imagination to envisage the thundering of hoofs, the clash of steel, and the bloody scene made famous in Tennyson's poem 'The Charge of the Light Brigade'.

Crimea is a magical place. Flying back, I remembered reading of the life of Prince Potemkin preparing for the visit of Empress Catherine in 1787. He arranged for many gardeners from England to create a glorious landscape, including gardens under glass—another example of British-Russian heritage.

6

ESTONIA

The Two Estonias

Meeting Alexander Volohhonski for the first time over a fine dinner in Tallinn, he said, "There are two Estonias—Russian Estonia and Estonia."

It was a challenging remark, but I came to gradually experience what he meant. Historically, Estonia had been part of the Danish, Swedish, and finally the Russian Empires before finally going independent in 1918. Then, during World War II, it was overrun by the Germans before being annexed into the Soviet Union in 1940.

Actually, over the period I spent in Estonia, I made great friends with both Russian Estonians and ethnic Estonians. And by and large, I felt little tension between them.

I owe my first visit to Tallinn to Andrew Rosindell, MP for Romford. In 1998, he had rung me to ask whether I would be free the following weekend to address the International Young Conservatives conference in Tallinn as the main speaker had just pulled out. At first I thought he said "Australia" and wondered how I was going to get there and be refreshed enough to deliver a keynote speech. But I was quickly assured that Estonia was in northern Europe and just a few hours away.

We arrived in Tallinn about 7 p.m., and I discovered my speech was scheduled almost immediately, at the opening dinner of the conference. I can't remember much of what I said, only that it was with relief that I sat down to a round of applause and a stiff drink. Seated next to me was the then prime minister, Mart Laar, who to my surprise asked me if I had a cigar. I luckily had two, and we smoked them over further wine. I had learned something from Alex Volohhonski, understanding that Mr Laar was a convinced Estonian Nationalist, who left me in no doubt as to his perceptions of Russian Estonians.

Mart Laar introduced me to his close friend Jaanus Reisner,, who asked me if it would be possible to arrange for the prime minister to visit Margaret Thatcher. By now, Lady Thatcher was retired, but despite the fact that for some reason the Conservative Central Office had not been keen on this visit, I felt it was worth asking her.

Actually, Lady Thatcher *was* keen on the idea which led to two meetings. The first was at her private

Eastern Encounters

residence in Kensington. I had briefed Laar that Margaret Thatcher was no fan of the European Union and that this would eventually be touched on. As we arrived, she greeted him with, "And why, Mr Laar, would you leave one union [meaning the Soviet Union] to join another [meaning the European Union]?" To which he instantly replied, "For the money!"

6. The author introducing Mart Laar to Margaret Thatcher, London 2002.

The second meeting was at a dinner during which Lady Thatcher had Vera Protosova, the Russian artist, at one side and Mart Laar on the other. Lady Thatcher spent some time enthusing about her visit to Moscow and the tremendous welcome she received only to hear her husband's booming voice call out, "Margaret, remember Prime Minister Laar is Estonian."

I remember reflecting that Margaret's great strength arose from both her firm and clear convictions and her readiness to communicate with others. She was able to both empathise with Russian Vera and Estonian Mart with natural ease.

On the day after my speech and meeting with Prime Minister Laar, I awoke to a crisp sunny morning. Following a hearty breakfast, I decided on an early exploration of Tallinn. Struck by the pealing of bells, I was naturally drawn to their source, the amazing St Alexander Nevsky Cathedral which reigns supreme over the old town. A stiff upwards walk along the mediaeval cobbled streets and numerous steps, and I finally arrived at the magnificent cathedral. I was amazed to see the number of people attending the liturgy on a Saturday morning. As I stepped very quietly inside, I found myself before the right-side altar, where a priest stood, awaiting penitents for confession. He beckoned me. Fortunately, by his side was a younger man who whispered in English, "Father Victor[18] was expecting you."

I was astonished! My first unexpected visit to

---

[18] Fr Victor Martyshkin.

Tallinn, and I was expected by this venerable priest. What happened next left a lasting impression. Father Victor disappeared for a few moments into the altar area before returning with a cross and chain, that he instantly placed round my neck. "This cross has been waiting for you on the altar for three days and will protect you, especially from any enemies," he said liberally sprinkling me with holy water before disappearing again in to the altar area. I turned to the young man who explained that Father Victor had supernatural gifts and that he had been privileged to witness such a scene. If he was privileged, I was astonished and left the cathedral in a state of near euphoria!

Soon I was back down to earth. JaanusReisner had very kindly offered to drive me into the Estonian countryside, so off we set on the Narva Road through beautiful forests gleaming in the sunny, snowy landscape. Something told me not to mention my experience in the cathedral to Jaanus. My instinct told me he might not be too impressed.

After several hours, we arrived at a small restaurant in the middle of a forest. Unassuming from the outside, it was warm and cosy inside, complete with roaring log fire. Seated at a window table, fine fare, vodka in hand, and falling snow outside, I lifted my glass to Jaanus and the wonderful Russian atmosphere. Poor Jaanus was not amused and corrected me: "This is not Russia. Now you are in Estonia."

Michael Wynne-Parker

The Old Town

After the first impressive visit, I made several trips to Tallinn. I was also struck by the obvious commercial opportunities in a country emerging from communism. Based on my successful start in Moscow, I decided to explore these in depth.

To this end, I rented a suite in the then named Grand Hotel, and for about a year, I used this as my base. I was fortunately joined in this exploratory venture by three friends—Fred Bristol,[19] Steve Metcalfe, and Toby Stone. Fred and Toby were principally interested in property opportunities and Steve in forestry. Over some months, we each secured apartments in the Old Town area within easy walking distance of each other.

Just before moving out of the hotel, the manager asked me if I would mind allowing someone to use my suite for a weekend, knowing that I would be away in the United Kingdom. I readily agreed and packed away private items in a bedroom cupboard. I was told that the suite was to be occupied by Donald Rumsfeld,[20] and his security would be tight. Apparently he was woken in the night by a muffled sound coming from the locked cupboard. All hell broke loose, and Rumsfeld was rushed to safety. Finally, a key to the cupboard was

---

[19] Frederick William Augustus Hervey, 8th Marquess of Bristol.
[20] US Secretary of Defense, 1932–2021.

found, and my alarm clock was discovered to be the culprit!

Despite our hectic search to discover appropriate business projects, we four expats began to enjoy the magical world of Tallinn Old Town. It was a unique atmosphere. For centuries, the Danes, Swedes, and Russians had preserved it as a capital for the elite. Hence the amazing preservation of its ancient houses, churches, and other buildings. Traders came and went, but a stillness preserved the homes of the Germanic merchant class, who lived comfortable lives in gracious surroundings.

Old Town is particularly attractive in winter under snow and perfect peace without tourists. In the first years, cultural tourists arrived in the late spring, enjoying the newly opened restaurants round the old square and the numerous antique shops and second-hand bookshops. You never knew what you would find in those shops. One day I spotted a pastel in an oval frame of a familiar face. It was Rasputin[21], looking straight at me with mesmerizing eyes. On closer examination, I realised it was an original frame, and scratched upon the back was his distinctive signature. I later had it authenticated. He was the man credited with bringing down the House of Romanov and consequently, the Russian Empire. Interesting to imagine how it had

---

[21] Grigory Rasputin, 1869–1916.

arrived from St Petersburg to Tallinn. Interesting too was the reaction of President Meri,[22] who was shocked to see it hanging in my Tallinn residence. "You know he has evil influence," said the president, to which I responded, "Yes, I know. But he has been blessed with the rest of the house, so no harm can come." For indeed my mysterious friend from Alexander Nevsky Cathedral had visited the place soon after my moving in, and Father Victor had given Rasputin an extra-liberal sprinkling of holy water.

Yes, in those early days, we were privileged to experience the all-pervading cultural atmosphere of old Tallinn before the hordes arrived.

Firstly came the stag parties. These were largely groups of extremely rowdy men intent on getting drunk and making a general nuisance of themselves, especially with the local girls. Now to be clear, we four single friends were not unaware of the numerous beautiful single ladies seen in every street and in every restaurant, not to mention the increasing number of nightclubs and bars. Indeed, we were fortunate to meet compatible girlfriends and potential wives. The problem with the stags was that they were here today and gone tomorrow, which seemed to imply total lack of responsibility. Finally, the police were instructed to take action. I remember one Sunday morning watching a couple

---

[22] President of Estonia 1929–2006.

Eastern Encounters

of semi-naked chaps being thrown into the back of a police van. They would be held in custody until fully sober, almost certainly missing their scheduled flights. I wonder how they would have explained this to wives and families.

Perhaps more impactful were the sudden invasions of massive cruise ships. Locals well remember the first one entering Tallinn harbour—a vast, ugly vessel causing waves to lap into the surrounding streets. Then out poured thousands of so-called tourists in groups of fifty, each led by someone holding a flag aloft. The streets were suddenly jammed as the tourists marched through like some vast invading horde, making it impossible for ordinary residents to walk the footpaths. Sadly, such was their limited time ashore that local gift shops profited little. Restaurants profited not at all, for after all the disruption, the horde would disappear back on to their cruise ship for a luxury lunch to prepare them for their next invasion into St Petersburg.

Otherwise, life in Tallinn was peaceful, enjoyable, and conducive to productive work for now we were entering the digital age. Great progress could be made via computer and laptop, impossible just a few years before.

In fact, Estonia was rapidly becoming a technological world leader, famous, for example, for developing Skype and TransferWise. Its banking system was also way ahead of that in the United Kingdom, with instant bank transfers instead of cheques and instant investment facilities online. Before I knew where I was, I was buying and selling gold purely via the banking app without any broker or paperwork. This was initially quite a shock and then unheard of in England. Very quickly a multitude of old-fashioned banks which had emerged in late Soviet times were now amalgamated into well-known names such as SEB and Hansabank.

It was very interesting to contrast my life in Tallinn with my UK life, and somehow I needed both. Over the next few years, I spent the majority of my time in Estonia with frequent short trips to London and Moscow.

To London I would fly direct for a very pleasant two hours. There were few passengers but attentive attendants with delicious food and wines, a far cry from today. Of course, I avoided Friday flights from London once the stag parties began!

To Moscow I would travel by train. This was a very pleasant discovery in early 2003 and became my regular method of travel. A magical journey. I always ordered a single-occupancy carriage. There was a spacious, comfortable berth with crisp bedsheets and a table large enough to enjoy a bottle of wine whilst in the summer months, enjoying views of sunlit meadows and endless forest.

Once, however, I had a shock. Having settled in, the door opened, and in came a pleasant but talkative older woman. After an hour of endless chatter, I discreetly persuaded the attendant to allocate another coupe for me, which she kindly did after we departed Narva, and there was no danger of any other passengers joining the now non-stop train to Moscow. No sooner was I tucking into my picnic supper than came a knock at the door, and the same woman appeared. I had left my book behind. Now what to do? I was about to offer a glass of wine when, rather thankfully, she said she was delighted to get to sleep alone.

Fire

Having enjoyed his first visit to Ukraine, it did not take too much to persuade HRH Prince Michael to visit Estonia. In fact, during my time there, he visited twice.

The first visit was in May 2002. Initially the idea was to explore the possibility of establishing a branch of the Children's Fire and Burns Trust,[23] of which HRH was patron, and I had been a supporter. The Trust had done splendid work within the United Kingdom and was now poised to expand its operations abroad. Already I had established contact with the Estonian Fire and Rescue Service and a hospital specialising in serious burn complications in children.

---

[23] Now called Children's Burns Trust.

We combined business with pleasure. One Monday, 6 May, we first visited Keila Hospital, where Prince Michael made a great impression on severely afflicted children, one who, peering through her heavily bandaged face, really thought Father Christmas had come to visit her!

Next we visited the headquarters of the Estonia Fire and Rescue Service and came to appreciate how intertwined fire rescue and serious injuries are. At the time in the United Kingdom, ambulances and fire engines were two separate entities; in Estonia, they operated as one unit. After these two visits, we were clear that the work and experience of the Children's Fire and Burns Trust could be very helpful in Estonia.

Actually, just a few weeks later, I was to have personal experience with the rescue service. I had a serious accident skidding across a wet tiled bathroom in the Grand Hotel, resulting in an involuntary rendition of the splits! I managed to pull an emergency rope which initially brought a manager to the suite. In turn, he called the Fire and Rescue Service. Minutes later, I received a jab which relieved the unbearable pain, and with a heave, my legs were back where they should be. I was later taken to a specialist unit and given magnetic therapy, that had been developed in Soviet times for disabled athletes. After the experience of successful treatment, I became a firm supporter of the Fire and

Rescue Service and prepared a fundraising campaign under, of course, the Fire and Burns Trust.

Thus came about Prince Michael's second and rather more high-profile visit. We decided to hold a fundraising ball in the perfect setting of the historical Kadriorg Palace, built by Peter the Great, and the summer residence of Nicholas II, Prince Michael's great-uncle.

This second visit was to be a three-day event in 2003 and attracted support from far and wide. Indeed, major sponsors included a group of Trust supporters who flew over from the United States and were very generous donors.

Though President Meri had now been succeeded by President Ruutel, who would officially attend the ball, I decided to ring President Meri to see if he would like a private visit from Prince Michael. I proposed lunch on Saturday, 19 March. "How did you know it will be my birthday?" responded the amazed former president. "And nothing would give me greater pleasure.' Thus, both the prince and the former president afforded each other great pleasure. All of us taking part enjoyed every minute for President Meri had spared no expense or trouble with a sumptuous luncheon in his charming residence overlooking the sea.

7. With Lennart Meri, former president of Estonia, Tallinn, 2003.

There was not a lot of recovery time after the luncheon before proceeding to the miniature but magnificent Kadriorg palace. It was like stepping back into the nineteenth century with blazing chandeliers, elegant dress, champagne, and a perfect string orchestra. President Arnold Ruutel arrived with the first lady. I had wondered about language as the president spoke little English and Prince Michael no Estonian. Then to my amazement, the president addressed the prince

Eastern Encounters

in Russian, that he speaks fluently. And all was well—despite at least one overheard remark to the effect that Russian is not the most popular language in Estonia.

8. Carolyn Cripps, HRH Prince Michael of Kent, President and Madam Arnold Ruutel, The Children's Fire and Burns Trust Kadriorg Ball, 2003.

The ball was not only enjoyable and memorable but also a great success financially due to generous support not only from the American guests but from local sponsors eager both to meet Prince Michael and support a very worthy cause. I had long before learned that the best way to raise funds for charity is to introduce potential donors to royalty. It works every time!

Despite the long and happy night, Prince Michael was keen to attend the liturgy the next day (Sunday) in Alexander Nevsky Cathedral. And once again, we witnessed the effect on the congregants who could hardly help but notice the prince's resemblance to the martyred tsar.

9. HRH Prince Michael of Kent with HE Metropolitan Cornelius, St Alexander Nevsky Cathedral, Tallinn, 2003.

As a result of our luncheon with former president Meri, I received a call from him inviting me to another lunch, this time in the historic Gloria Restaurant. It had survived from imperial times through Soviet times to the present day. The president was very curious to hear

Eastern Encounters

all about the ball, especially how his successor handled the occasion. After telling him about the ball, he went on to tell me about one of his great interests, the story of the meteorite which landed on the island of Saaremaa.[24] This was about 3,500 years ago and had obviously made a huge impression on local folk history. :Legend has it that the dramatic light effects could be seen far away in surrounding countries. For hundreds of miles around, shards of metal penetrated the earth and were being discovered, according to ancient records, thousands of years later. Some of these iron pieces may have been used to create ancient iron crosses, such as those described in Eric Koats and Heinig Valks's fascinating book, *Cross and Iron*, revealing that the sacred image was known in Estonia twenty-five centuries ago!

President Meri had proposed a theory that Saaremaa was the legendary Thule Island, first mentioned by the Greek geographer Pytheas. He proposed the name Thule could have been connected to the Finnic word *tule* ("of fire") and the folklore of Estonia which depicts the birth of the crater lake in Kaali. The president believed that the meteorite incident led to local belief that Kaali was the place where, "The sun went to rest."

---

[24] Creating what became known as the Kaali crater

Magical Manors

In early 2002, I received an invitation to lunch with HRH Princess Michael of Kent. She had already been impressed and interested in Prince Michael's accounts of his visits to Tallinn and expressed a keen interest to see something of Estonia for herself.

Thus, on Sunday, 15 September, she arrived at Tallinn Airport to be received by the then British ambassador Sarah Squire. We had a cosy supper that evening in the vaulted dining room of the Schlossle Hotel, where the princess was staying. She was especially interested in the manor houses built in the eighteenth century by the so-called Baltic barons, who were largely attached to the Court of St Petersburg. In fact, I had recently acquired such a house, Khilevere Manor, in north-east Estonia, that Prince Michael had already visited. The princess has a good knowledge of architecture, so next day we set off with appropriate police escorts to view various houses and estates. She took copious notes, and to this day, I have the copy of *A Guide to Manor Houses in Estonia* full of her interesting observations. It was her practical eye that convinced me to sell Khilevere. "Far too big, and how will you heat all these rooms in winters often freezing under 25 degrees Fahrenheit?" It was interesting that none of my male friends had made that observation.

Perhaps the most memorable moment was our visit to

Eastern Encounters

Lugvalla Manor. Unfortunately, we were not expected, and the house was closed. Turning to Inspector Jeremy Woolger, Princess Michael instructed, "Shoot the lock." Nothing like a royal command to do the trick.

Ever since Princess Michael's visit, I have read and enjoyed her historical books. She has shrewd powers of observation, making her books impossible to put down. I like to think that her experience of the unique manor houses in Estonia played at least a small part.

I was in the bar of the Grand Hotel when the news came of the US-led invasion of Iraq. Next to me was a reporter for the main Estonian TV channel,[25] who asked for my reaction. From the beginning, I was against Bush's so-called war on terror and the unholy alliance he struck with Tony Blair. I told this to the reporter in no uncertain manner. He asked if I would do an interview for that evening's news; I accepted with alacrity. This was my first Estonian TV appearance. Despite many Estonians having a reasonable regard for both the United States and the United Kingdom, I was amazed at how much support I received following my forthright public dismissal of the notorious foreign intervention. Among them was a positive call from former president Meri. That same evening, I was invited to a party given by increasingly well-known sculptor Tarno Kangro. Included at the party were Ander Ild

---
[25] ETV

and his fiancée, Hannah, an acclaimed singer. All had just seen my TV appearance, and I was encouraged by their general responses. Ander and Hannah became close friends, giving me over time privileged insight into real Estonian life. They also shared a love of Estonian manors and in due course decided on the one they would devote their life and resources to—Neeruti Manor. Today the house and its considerable gardens are magnificently restored.

    I well remember visiting Neeruti with Hannah and Ander one early spring day. It was originally known as Buxhowden in the glorious days of the Baltic barons, back in the days of Empress Catherine.[26] But now it lay in ruins, and the park with a river running through it utterly overgrown. As though inspired by a vision of restoration, we began to make the drive, pull up weeds, and attack the advancing thick undergrowth with shears and knives. But alas, little impression was made, and within the great entrance hall, bits of the formerly grand staircase hung from crumbling walls. But visions can come true, and today, just a few years later, Neeruti stands not just intact but glamorously and sensitively restored. It is a home again and not only perfected within. Its park and gardens flourish with shrubs, plants, flowers, and vegetables amidst the ancient trees. And most significantly, the gardens

---

[26] Catherine II, known as Catherine the Great 1729-1796

are organic; no chemical fertilisers or pesticides here. The results amazing to behold. Well done, Ander and Hannah!

10. With Ander and Hannah Ild, first visit to Neeruti Manor, Estonia, 2004.

Soon after meeting Ander and Hannah, Fred Bristol and I received an invitation to their wedding, that was indeed the Estonian wedding of the year. Apart from the joy of witnessing a celebration of true love, we were plunged into fascinating Estonian traditional life. On arriving at the Lutheran Cathedral, it was unnoticeable that all the guests held large bouquets of flowers which, at the end of the ceremony, were presented to the happy bride and groom. We were slightly embarrassed to be the only ones without, but a large smile seemed to do the trick, and soon we were on our way in a convoy of 40 Mercedes to the next surprise, a presentation at Palme Manor.

It was an enactment of a mythological story around the lake where we, the lucky guests, stood enthralled. Hannah walked slowly towards the water's edge on the far bank to whisper her name to the wind, a symbolic giving up of her name in exchange for Ander's. Then strode forth our hero with a great sword to take his bride in triumph. I later discovered that the sword had been made by Tarno Kangro. The hilt was made from one of Peter the Great's oak trees. No escape from the Russians!

From these magical moments, the convoy sped to Kalvi Manor for the evening banquet and dancing. I had written a poem which I was asked to read at the beginning of dinner. The poem related to my meeting with Hannah and Ander with Tarno on the evening of my TV appearance and appropriate thanks to Saddam. At the end of dinner, Hannah and Ander together sang a lovely Frank Sinatra rendition, and their radiant happiness cast a spell on all present. Finally, I went to sleep at 5 a.m. to be wakened by Fred at 12:50, announcing that departure was in ten minutes.

It is friends rather than actual places that make life meaningful. With the combination of growing friendships and Tallinn's rich cultural heritage, plus a growing number of first-class restaurants, life in

Estonia was very pleasant. I also liked the seasonal contrasts, real winters of frost and thick snow followed by hot, long summer days.

Pühtitsa

His Eminence Metropolitan Cornelius was an outstanding personality. It was significant that the head of the Russian Orthodox Church in Tallinn was an Estonian, and he, therefore, played an important role in easing ethnic tensions.

After the death of his wife, he had taken monastic vows and quickly succeeded Alexi II, who had been elected Patriarch of the Russian Orthodox Church, as Metropolitan of Tallinn and All Estonia.

It was with great pleasure that I was honoured to receive him for lunch on 9 July 2004. Walking into my library, he exclaimed, *"War and Peace,"* which I did not understand until much later, when he described a scene in a Russian version of the great book with an almost identical room. I decided to prepare everything myself. We had a simple lunch of fish, curried eggs, salad, cheese, and red wine—all of which I had checked in advance would be to his liking.

I discovered a deeply philosophical man ready to embrace and offer his amazing insight to all. I was quickly struck by his profound observation, "There is no such thing as an evil man, only a mistaken one." It was a theme he often touched on in his Sunday sermons. He had no time for petty religious prejudices or narrow concepts. And above all, he lived what he preached. It was his eightieth birthday about then, and I gave him a book depicting Jerusalem, Mount Athos, and Russian churches abroad given to me by Archimandrite Count Anthony Grabbe in 1970.

It was Metropolitan Cornelius who suggested I visit the Pühtitsa Convent. I asked Fred Bristol if he would like to join me on a first-day visit, a three-hour drive from Tallinn through heavily wooded country in eastern Estonia, close to the Russian border. It is always amazing to see the traditional onion-shaped domes suddenly appearing on the skyline amidst the surrounding forest as if by magic.

On arrival, we were met by Mother Tikhona, the librarian. In perfect English, she warmly welcomed us and took us round the convent complex of six churches, beautiful gardens, and impressive domestic quarters. She explained that according to legend, a shepherd from the village of Kaemae witnessed a divine revelation near a spring of water. Later in the sixteenth century, locals found an ancient icon at the very spot, under a huge oak tree. It was an icon of the Dormition of the Mother of God. It is in the main church of the convent to this day and after which the convent is named.

In 1888, the building of the present convent began in traditional Russian Revival style; it was formally consecrated in 1910. The convent survived the two world wars despite the battlefront in the Second World War being at times only a few kilometres away, and a concentration camp for Russian prisoners was actually within the convent compound.

We were received for lunch by the legendary Abbess Varvara, who was proud to be in charge of a now thriving community of over 160 nuns. It was one of only two monastic communities which survived and flourished during the period of the Soviet Union.[27] She told a remarkable story. One day a German arrived and told the abbess that he had been sent on a flying mission to bomb the convent. As he approached the area, thick clouds completely hid the entire complex, and his bomb fell into a neighbouring field. He had been privately very relieved, and thus years later, had returned to tell the tale and ask forgiveness, which the abbess, amazed at his honesty and bravery, readily gave.

Since that first visit, I have returned many times, twice staying for several days to absorb the special atmosphere of peace and holy quiet. Impressive is the daily discipline of the sisters, who are encouraged to use their natural talents whether as cooks, gardeners, farmers, or singers in the choir at the daily services. Yes, the convent is completely self-contained and self-sufficient. Delicious seasonal meals are derived from

---

[27] The other is the Pskov Caves monastery just over the Russian border.

the extensive gardens, orchards, and farm. A doctor, nurses, and an infirmary for the very old are part of the complex. I also met several nuns who had permission to serve in the wider world as teachers and lecturers in European and Russian universities.

Once a year, the peace and quiet is disturbed—very positively—by the Feast of the Dormition ceremonies.[28] These begin with a festive liturgy presided over by the Metropolitan, who has his own house within the complex, followed by a procession of several thousands to the Holy Spring, where the faithful are thoroughly sprinkled with the sacred water. A festive lunch follows for about one hundred invited guests, whilst the majority enjoy picnics all around. Amazingly, each time I have been present, the sun has shone.

The experiences at Pühtitsa led me to visit several monasteries in different parts of Russia. Over eight hundred have emerged since the end of the communist period, an amazing sign of a general spiritual renaissance in the Russian sphere.

During my first experience of the Dormition feast at Pühtitsa, I had the pleasure of meeting Ksenia and Thomas Havvistu. I quickly discovered that Ksenia is the granddaughter of Metropolitan Cornelis, and I was keen to gain insights into the character of the man I had come to admire so much.

---

[28] Celebrated on the 15th August each year

Eastern Encounters

Soon after our first meeting, Ksenia and Thomas kindly asked me to visit their home in southern Estonia, a remote and beautiful part of the country I had not seen before. It was during this visit that we went to see the mausoleum in which lie the embalmed bodies of Barclay de Tolly and his wife at Jogeveste. Of course, Barclay is a famous name in Norfolk, where much of my life is spent, and I had becomeaware of the Barclay[29] family's connections to the illustrious Barclay de Tolly in conversation with Rupert Barclay.

11. Barclay de Tolly Mausoleum, Jogeveste, Estonia, 2004.

---
[29] Rupert Barclay of Hanworth, Norfolk.

As mentioned earlier, Estonia is famous for its many manor houses established by the so-called Baltic barons, who served the court of St Petersburg. Barclay de Tolly descended from Clan Barclay of Towic Castle, Aberdeenshire, who intermarried into German nobility; some of whom became Baltic barons. Barclay entered the Russian military, wherein his rapid rise brought him to the attention of Tsar Alexander 1. He went on to play a significant role in the Russo-Swedish war of 1808–1809, that resulted in the incorporation of Finland into the Russian Empire. Consequently, he was appointed governor general of Finland. Later, as head of the Ministry of Military Affairs, Barclay contributed greatly to the increased efficiency of the Russian Army and intelligence ability. This was timely as Napoleon was about to begin his famous but ultimately disastrous invasion of 1812, so memorably captured in Russian culture by Tchaikovsky's music and Tolstoy's writings.

It was Barclay de Tolly who persuaded famous Mikhail Kutuzov[30] to pursue a defensive scorched-earth strategy which, though very unpopular, ultimately led to Napoleon's inglorious retreat from the Russian lands. After Kutuzov's death, Barclay succeeded him as commander-in-chief, and in 1814, led a detachment into Paris, forcing Napoleon's abdication.

Standing before the impressive classical mausoleum

---

[30] General Prince Mikhail Kutusov, 1745–1813.

with my two Estonian friends, I saluted the memory of this amazing man, and the German, Russian-Estonian, Scottish, and Norfolk links.

Majesty

Life was never dull in Tallinn. On 18 November 2004, I invited Ander Ild to lunch at the Schlössle Hotel, a belated birthday treat for him. Peter Knoll, then general manager, joined us for a few minutes, announcing that a distinguished visitor was about to arrive—the president of Bulgaria. I asked, "Do you really mean the prime minister? What is his name?"

Peter replied, "Something unpronounceable."

I asked, "Is it Saxe-Coberg Gotha?" to which he answered it was. Then to Ander's surprise, I replied, "Peter, you don't have the president arriving but the prime minister! And you should address him as His Majesty." I went on to explain how Simeon, for that is his first name, was the first man ever to have been crowned a king—actually, tsar of the Bulgarians—at the age of five and now, years later, to be the democratically elected prime minister.

This revelation, of course, made a great impression on Peter, stirring general excitement throughout the hotel. I left my card for Simeon, scribbling on it that Frederick is also in Tallinn. Not too surprisingly, I received a telephone call during the evening inviting

Michael Wynne-Parker

both Fred and me to visit him in Bulgaria. This did not happen as Simeon lost the next election. So much better to be a king.

I originally met King Simeon with Victor Bristol, Fred's father, in London many years before. I visited him several times since in both London and Madrid, where he lived permanently in exile.

I was not taken by surprise by the next distinguished visitor to Tallinn because I arranged it. Count Nikolai Tolstoy[31] has been a friend for many years and agreed to visit with Georgina, his wife, to give a talk at a meeting of the English-Speaking Union held at Kadriorg Palace. Nikolai was keen on the visit partly because of his family connections both with Russia and the Baltic States.

The very name Tolstoy speaks for itself, especially to Slavic ears. Word quickly spread that the great man was in town to make a speech. The magnificent main hall of the palace was filled to standing room only. After speaking, Nikolai answered questions for almost an hour. Very aptly in the context of the English-Speaking Union, and aware of the underlying tensions between the Estonians and Estonian Russians, Nikolai stressed

---

[31] Count Nikolai Dmitriev Tolstoy-Miloslavsky, current nominal head of the House of Tolstoy: Author of many books including 'Victims of Yalta' 1977; 'Stalin's Secret War' 1981; 'The Tolstoys - 24 Generations of Russian History' 1983; 'The Minister and the Massacres' 1986; 'The Coming of the King' 1988.

the importance of a common language—in this case English—to allow communication and thus bridge the cultural divide.

12. Count Nikolai Tolstoy, Kadriorg Palace, 2007.

Among those attending the Tolstoy lecture was George Kirilov. I had first met George in Alexander Nevsky Cathedral and was at once struck by his Rasputin-like presence with his seemingly all-seeing eyes. Those eyes looked deeply into the eyes of all he met for he was a poet, and observation is the essence of real poetry. Each Sunday after liturgy, we would drink coffee in a local bar, in the summer outside where tourists would stop, and he would sign and sell them a book of his poems. In the winter, all tourists gone, we sat inside, and I learned much from George about his experience as a Russian living in Tallinn from the last years of the Soviet period. He impressed on me that in those early days, money did not exist as the state covered almost everything. Family conversation centred on cultural themes rather than material things. But George was no socialist. In fact, he was an ardent monarchist, that I was beginning to understand was not uncommon amongst Russians. He constantly asked me to arrange a visit to London.

The opportunity came when George's first English edition was published in the summer of 2004. It is titled *The Silvery Smell of Coffee* and was translated by Richard McKane, who I had come across in London. Poetry is not easy to translate, but Richard completely immersed himself in George's work, entering the world of imagination which lay behind the words, Nikolai Tolstoy aptly summed this up, stating, "I have greatly enjoyed reading Georgy Kirilov's poems. They are carefully crafted, touching and illusive and deserve to be widely read by the discriminating."

Here are the opening verses:

> The silvery smell of coffee,
> grey eyes of Spring,
> unintentionally, in passing,
> the word 'we' was let fall.

> Blindness raised the wall
> but there's a day and an hour for everything.
> At the sunset hour we are able
> to find our road to Damascus.

The book is beautifully illustrated by a talented but anonymous surrealist Tallinn artist.

Already a few London visitors to George's website were anxious to meet the great man. Luckily, one of those was Julian Gallant, then director of Pushkin House, London. After weeks of preparation, George Kirilov took his first flight and enjoyed every minute of his first and only London experience, making an unforgettable impression on all he met. Our mutual friend, Juri,[32] had enthusiastically agreed to accompany and look after George, who greatly appreciated being based at Windsor. From there they arrived at Pushkin House, where a large number of George's fans—old and new—were treated to an enjoyable and inspirational poetry reading. What a challenge for George to read his work in English to a live audience for the first time!

For many, George was a man of mysteries and difficult to understand, even to those in the Russian community. To me, he worthily represented the finest tradition of the St Petersburg poets—Anna Akhmatova, Sergey Eoenin, and Marina Tsvetaeva. Yet in private, he admitted that he particularly loved the American

---

[32] Juri Pavlov

poets Robert Frost and amazingly my own favourite, Dorothy Parker—no relation!

13. With George Kirilov, Tallinn, 2007.

In October 2005, came HRH Princess Katarina of Yugoslavia to Tallinn. Of course, this particularly pleased George. I have known Katarina since her teenage years as her father, Prince Tomislav, was a close friend. She is by nature an enthusiast and took little persuasion to embark on a three-day tour. This created great interest amongst both the Estonian and Russian communities, probably because Katarina is related to both Russian and German royal families, as well as most of the royal families of Europe as a direct descendant of

Queen Victoria. Naturally, the visit began in Tallinn, including a reception at the Town Hall attended by many local dignitaries.

14. HRH Princess Katarina of Yugoslavia visiting Tallinn City Hall with Toomas Vitsut, HE Metropolitan Cornelius, and me, 2005.

Memorable was our lunch aboard the *Admiral*, berthed in Tallinn harbour. This had been suggested by Metropolitan Cornelius as the owners of the vessel[33] are Serbian and delighted to welcome their very own princess of Yugoslavia! His Eminence the Metropolitan presided over a sumptuous Serbian lunch

---

[33] Igor and Natalia Grojic

with vodka—in reasonable quantities, of course, as you can't possibly have drunken prelates and princesses!

After an informal tour of the Old Town, we had a delicious dinner at the Schlössle, joined by Fred Bristol as Prince Tomislav was Fred's godfather. We always called Prince Tomislav Tommy, and to him we raised a toast.

The next day we set off early to Rakvere, the capital of Laane-Viru County in north Estonia. Church bells and a small crowd welcomed us to the Church of the Nativity of the Mother of God, where Katarina was formally received by the mayor and local priest. The church is famous as it contains the remains of martyred priest Sergei Florenski, St Sergei (he was canonised in 2002), after a remarkable life as a teacher, brave soldier, and priest. He was arrested by the Red Army, and after a single brief interrogation, was executed in a neighbouring forest. It was a moving moment as we stood before his tomb in the centre of the church.

From Rakvere, we took a long drive to Pühtitsa Convent and a warm greeting from Abbess Varvara, who prepared a very welcome lunch. After lunch, Mother Tikhona gave us a rapid tour of the museum and cathedral and then finally to the holy well, where we all indulged liberally in the freezing holy water.

Eastern Encounters

15. From left to right, Juri Polyakov, HRH Princess Katarina of Yugoslavia, Mother Tikhona, Abbess Vavara, and Sergei Mannik, Pühtitsa, 2005.

Back to the car and on to Narva, the capital at the extreme eastern point of Estonia on the Russian border. Not only was this Katarina's first visit, it was also mine. It was dark on arrival, so we could not see the endless Soviet housing estates that encircle the old town.

Katarina's welcome was enthusiastic and warm. All seemed grateful that she had made the effort to travel so far. On our arrival, the mayor pointed out that this was the first royal visit since Alexander III in 1870.

16. HRH Princess Katarina of Yugoslavia arriving at Narva Cathedral, 2005.

So much had to be packed into so little time. After a press conference which Katarina, sometimes prompted by me, handled well, we proceeded to the ancient fort, impressive even in the gloom, and then an inspection of the museum, all at rapid pace. Finally, we climbed the endless stairs to the top of the fort to see the glittering lights of Russia just yards away across the Narva River. Katarina later admitted to me that she is scared of heights and didn't know how she made it.

And then on to Narva Cathedral, where the choir was in full flow as the princess was conducted around. A throne had been placed close to the altar, but she rightly decided to stand throughout. It was interesting to hear that both Katarina's forebears, Alexander III and Kaiser Wilhelm, had visited this place, the latter presenting a Protestant cross which is there to this day. One understood how highly symbolic Katarina's visit was as it represented all sides of the monarchical and political systems. Most moving was the hearty singing of the Russian Imperial Anthem.

Finally, a festive dinner was held in a local hotel attended by the local dignitaries of church and state. There were generous toasts and speeches. We departed for the long drive to Tallinn with a car full (and I mean *full*) of flowers. Suffering from an allergy, I began to sneeze. Luckily, the driver, who had also started sneezing, suggested we call at a local orphanage, where Katarina was able to distribute the flowers to an amazed night staff. With windows open and good fresh air, we continued happily to Tallinn, arriving at 2 a.m.

Thankfully, the next day's engagements began at noon with a reception at the parliament hosted by Vilja Saavisaar, leader of the Centre Party, followed by a visit to Alexander Nevsky Cathedral, one minute's walk away. Metropolitan Cornelius had organised a final luncheon before an exhausted but exhilarated Princess Katarina boarded her plane home to London.

On 20 November 2005, I celebrated my sixtieth birthday in Tallinn. It was a party to be remembered. Several friends from abroad arrived, including Nick Stalder from Frankfurt, who proclaimed he was in charge. He had arranged two enormous pre-poached salmon (not a joke!), many other delicacies, and thirty bottles of champagne. He also arranged two waitresses, lovely girls in impeccable short skirts. Plus a young butler, who ensured all glasses were constantly full.

At midnight I heralded the moment of my sixtieth year on the hunting horn. Too early for going home, so a variation on the theme! Then came the magnificent cake made and decorated by Hannah, who composed the words inscribed thereon and then sang them. Father Juvenalius[34] then spoke and proposed a toast. His presence confused some "Is he Estonian?" Yes. "Of which church?" St Alexander Nevsky Cathedral. Surprise! An Estonian Russian Orthodox priest! It was interesting to reflect that of the fifty or so guests, about a third were Estonians, a third Estonian Russians, and a third of us outsiders. Yet all mingled and had a wonderful time.

On 20 October 2006, HM Queen Elizabeth II, accompanied by Prince Philip, made a two-day visit to Tallinn. Naturally, preparations were underway for months before, but very often important things are overlooked until the last minute. Queen Elizabeth and her party were to stay at the Three Sisters Hotel as it was the only one with a lift. The manager called me a few days before, asking if I would go round and check

---

[34] Fr Juvenalius Karma.

her suite. On arrival, I noticed that the bedroom had four magnificent picture frames on the walls but no pictures in them. This was a bit of the fashion at the time in renovated buildings. I told the manager that this would never do as the Queen had one of the most famous collections of fine works of art in the world. What to do? I proposed we go to the local museum and borrow four suitable pictures—naturally of horses and dogs—which quickly graced the walls.

Next, the bathroom. There was a large picture of a naked woman not at all suitable for a royal grandmother. It was also replaced with a horse. Finally, inspiration. The only reading materials in the suite were Estonian magazines. These I replaced with copies of *Country Life* magazine and for good measure, a couple of English books. One was a book given to me long ago by Patricia Bowes Lyon, a cousin of the Queen, and signed by her. And, of course, a copy of my recently published book *Reflections in Middle Years*. Rather a bold move, I thought. And so too did Prince Philip, who remarked, "You never miss a chance, Wynne-Parker." Actually, Prince Philip had read my first book, *Bridge over Troubled Water*, and taken the trouble to write a perceptive and an encouraging thank-you letter treasured to this day.

Michael Wynne-Parker

Fragile Union

Growingly conscious that I had good friends on both sides of the Estonian-Russian divide, I thought it a good plan to establish a branch of the English-Speaking Union. I had been impressed by the impact the ESU had in Sri Lanka, where the island is similarly divided by Sinhalese and Tamils. I had discovered that speaking a common language—English—could bridge the gap.[35] And I had discovered that most Estonians and Russians greatly desired to speak English.

Toomas Vitsut[36] was chairman of the Tallinn Council and had kindly introduced me to several interesting locals. He readily agreed to become the first chairman of the Estonian ESU. He presided over the first meeting, 1 February 2007, in Tallinn Town Hall. About eighty attended, of which thirty joined by signing an application form. *Not a bad start,* I thought. Toomas invited me to see all sectors of the somewhat divided society enjoying wine and refreshments together at the end of the gathering.

On the surface, everything seemed calm in Tallinn in the spring of 2007. There had been rumours, however, of disquiet. On 20 February, President Ilves was in London, and I found myself addressing him

---

[35] Hence the title of my book *Bridge Over Troubled Water*.
[36] Toomas Vitsut. Born 1960. Former member of Estonian parliament and chairman of Tallinn City Council since 2005.

thus: "Now, sir, you are a statesman." I had become aware that he had recently refused to sign an act of parliament to remove a monument to the fallen of the Second World War in central Tallinn. Apparently, this had been proposed by a group of influential Estonian Nationalists who, or whose parents, had been on the side of Germany. Of course, all Russians wished to retain it. It would have been inappropriate of me to make much of the British cooperation with "Uncle Joe", but beastly though he was, we were on the same side. So President Ilves had taken, in my opinion, the right stand, but he was not to prevail.

On Sunday evening 22 April, I was in St Alexander Nevsky Cathedral when George Kirilov tapped me on the shoulder and asked me to walk with him to the Monument to the Unknown Soldier. I thought this strange but quickly realised something was afoot as we encountered hundreds of people quietly surrounding the monument, before which each laid a red rose. It was a stirring moment, and I realised I was witnessing something unusual. Nothing was said; all were almost reverent in attitude. I quietly slipped away.

Next morning I received a call from a very distressed Julia Jolkin, who was working with me at the time. She said she was too sick to work. She told me that at 4 a.m., the police had dispersed the huge crowd and moved the monument to a secret destination. Where the statue had stood was now a large tent surrounded by police.

Julia said, "I have learned Estonian, paid my taxes, integrated myself into Estonia, and now feel rebutted and devastated." This I was very shocked to hear.

Initially, calm still appeared in the town, and that evening, I had two guests to dinner, one Estonian and one Russian Estonian. Suddenly, the Estonian's mobile rang, and she answered, understanding things were not quite normal. It was her mother, who proclaimed that the Old Town was under attack by a violent mob. There was an uproar as shops and restaurants were being broken into and looted, and my friend should not venture out. Now, my house in the Old Town had extremely thick walls and was surrounded by a courtyard, so we could hear nothing of the chaos outside. We continued our dinner and tried to analyse the situation from Estonian, Russian, and British points of view.

The Estonian government had finally removed the statue of the Soviet soldier. Whilst to most Europeans—well, to British people at least—the monument represented the end of World War II. To many Estonians, it represented the Soviet occupation. One statue, two interpretations.

The fact that the operation to remove the statue happened at 4 a.m. in the morning had taken most people by surprise, adding to the angry reaction. And angry it was. At about 9 p.m., there were reports of fires and disturbances in the Old Town. These developed into a full-scale rebellion enveloping much of the city by midnight. Shop windows were smashed one after another, street by street. Looting of everything from pharmaceuticals to designer clothes, antiques, and jewellery added to the general chaos as thousands of young Russians stormed the area.

My two dinner guests were now so alarmed that they rang the police and were told to stay put. Thus they did until 6 a.m. Stella Wadowsky, a famous local journalist, rang me and made me promise not to venture out; she knows my curiosity streak. So I only opened the front door and looked out into Sauna Street. A young Estonian, walking alone, approached me and said, "Sir, please go inside. It is not safe. The mob is approaching." Suddenly, all hell was let loose in the neighbouring Muurivahe Street as antique and jewellery shops were ransacked. My new friend rang the police on his mobile, got through, and a few minutes later, a solitary police car emerged through the crowd which disbanded, some of them charging in Sauna Street. I and my friend rushed inside and locked the door until the disturbance quite quickly died down. I unlocked the door, and he left into the dark night. Upstairs, my guests were sleeping in my study. I decided to get some sleep as well.

Next morning I met Stella Wadowsky, and we actually found a table in about the only restaurant open. Neither of us could believe the turmoil around, and we tucked onto a good lunch despite being the only ones in the place. The looting of the previous night had been brought under control, and police were much in evidence, presiding over an eerie calm.

This strange atmosphere continued over the next day. The streets empty, no tourists. Where had they gone? Broken glass and debris everywhere. A ghost town indeed. I had arranged some time before the crisis to meet Father Victor at the cathedral before going on to lunch out of town with Ivan and Maria Klimenko. There were barricades everywhere, especially round the cathedral. However, I marched through them to find Father Victor completely unperturbed, and we drove off to an excellent lunch at which the subject of the crisis was not touched on at all—whether this was through politeness or just general relief to be away from it. We drank champagne, and Father Victor quoted huge chunks of Pushkin in an appropriately dramatic manner.

On our return to Tallinn, I at once noticed a difference. In the space of just a few hours, thousands of people now thronged the streets. I learned that they had been bussed in from all over Estonia and had come to stage a remarkable, but on the whole orderly, protest. The police seemed to have disappeared.

Where all those people stayed overnight was a mystery, but the next day, their numbers seemed to have dramatically increased. It was almost impossible to move at all in the streets. Despite this, Fred Bristol, Toby

Stone, and I decided to dine in one of the restaurants now reopened. We enjoyed a good dinner and agreed we would see what the crowds were up to. So we set off rather unwisely, cigars in hand, and soon found ourselves lost in the enormous throng which stretched as far as the eye could see. Chaos suddenly erupted as a large contingent of mounted police charged into the scattering crowd. Luckily, we knew the area and quickly made for a convenient high wall behind which we hid until the main thrust of the charge was over.

We hastily retreated via some side streets to the safety of my home, where we continued to puff our cigars in a state of amazement at what we just witnessed in normally tranquil Tallinn. On reflection, we agreed that on the whole, the crowds were good natured and only a few missiles—small rocks—had narrowly missed us. Clearly the aim of the exercise had been to move the crowds away from the centre of the Old Town. The following are my thoughts as recorded in my diary on 27 April 2007:

> There is no smoke without fire, and I think this fire is beginning to rage and will not easily be put out.
> Why?
> Various views are put forward by the local populace. For example one Estonian (cynic) said to me today, "It's simple, the

government want the land to sell to a construction company."

Of course, the official view is that the monument represents the dreadful Soviet past of which all reminders must be destroyed.

Now this is understandable. The Soviet regime was quite as dreadful as the Nazi regime, and the sufferings of the Estonians were terrible, including the thousands sent to Siberia.

Memories die hard. Many are still bitter and a minority very bitter indeed. It is only time, and in some cases business pragmatism, that heals these wounds. We British have long ago come to terms with the Germans and Japanese. This is not so with many Estonians in their attitude to Russians. Many Russians understand this, and with their generally generous nature, are sensitive to the feelings of their fellow Estonians. Other Russians, however, brood over their second-class citizenship (like the Palestinians in Israel and Tamils in Sri Lanka), and amongst them, the tensions have been gradually building up to finally explode today.

The monument issue is neither the only nor main issue; its removal symbolises to the Russian psyche a total disrespect for their own culture and identity.

The poorer and often less-educated Russian is deprived of a full passport. He is described as an alien. This is not believed by most Europeans. But it is true. And I believe it to be the first cause of today's outpouring of anger. The sooner all Estonians are given a full passport, i.e., citizenship, the better. This action could begin to diffuse the situation.

There is also a tremendous gap between the very rich and the poor in Estonia. I have witnessed this gap growing over my five years here and have become aware of the growing unrest it creates. There is little point in a country boasting of an increasingly successful economy if many of its citizens are not enjoying the benefits thereof. All civil wars thrive in an atmosphere of disadvantage, and Estonian leaders should concentrate on raising the economic standards of the working and professional classes.

It is difficult to see where today's demonstration will lead. I think matters will get worse until the government takes a sensitive and bold lead.

1) Place the monument in an appropriate situation with dignity, and encourage the people to see it as a symbol of the defeat of fascism rather than a symbol of Soviet oppression. This would take very great statesmanship, and I wonder whether the present leaders have the will and ability to rise to the occasion.
2) Give passports to all Estonians reducing to the absolute minimum the present language requirements. The rich can get an Estonian passport without Estonia language proficiency.
3) Make every effort to include the Russian people within the Estonian establishment with enthusiasm. Equally, Russians should welcome Estonians thus.
4) Make every effort to strengthen diplomatic ties with Russia, not just at a commercial level—which at present is more or less the only level, but also at a cultural and social level.
5) Develop maturity via self-confidence. Live for the present not the past, and reach out into the future to evolve a multicultural society where all can live and prosper in peace.

And this is an email sent the same day to Julia Belokurova in London:

Dear Julia,

You have probably already heard of the riots here. It started yesterday and became serious after dark when about 3,000 rampaged the streets, destroying shops, looting etc. The police simply could not cope. It died down about 5 a.m., and now everyone is just wandering about, unable to believe the carnage. Alcohol sales will be banned from 2 p.m. today, but I doubt that will do the trick as there is an angry mood in the air, and now the famous monument has been taken away to a yet unknown destination, a large part of the population are furious.

Speak soon,
M

As the years have passed, on the surface, at least things seem to have settled down. And, of course, a younger generation has a different perspective.

The monument was finally re-established in the Estonian Defence Forces Cemetery of Tallinn, though several bodies claimed by relatives were reburied in various places in Estonia and Russia.

Unfortunately, the issue of full passports has not been fully resolved, and many poorer Russians still have an alien's passport, known as 'grey passports'. An amazing situation in today's European Union!

I was surprised on 7 May to receive a call from Kristina Ojuland, Estonia's foreign minister, inviting me to a friendship dinner with invitees from both sides of the ethnic divide and others. Apart from myself, others included my dinner companion, Anna-Maria Golanyan, who clearly with Armenian blood, told me that she was Russian Orthodox and that her godmother was the famous Abbess Varvara. She also told me that she was head of the European Agency in Tallinn and would be delighted to receive me there.

As time went on, I learned that Anna-Maria was caught up in a growing scandal over EU funds and was ultimately arrested, charged, and imprisoned for six months. However, she was kind to me in making several introductions. By far, the most important was to Vladimir Volohhonski, father of Alexander, already referred to.

Anna-Maria first brought Vladimir to lunch on a fine summer's day. I was deeply impressed both by his humility, despite being one of Estonia's most successful businessmen, and his philosophical outlook. He was also a great philanthropist, very generously helping many causes, including building churches, developing the Tallinn Zoo, and supporting the Tallinn Football

Club. Indeed, later in 2009, he asked me to co-host an event for famous British football referee Howard Webb, whom I greatly enjoyed meeting and getting to know.

Another fascinating friend of Vladimir's was Alexander Mikhailov, a famous Russian actor who has appeared in forty-two films since 1973. I met him at one of Vladimir's enjoyable parties.

It is said that a single man in Tallinn will not remain single for long. There are so many attractive single women, many looking for an escape into another and wider world. I was divorced and free and delighted to meet Jelena Sahharova through our mutual friend, Stella Wadowsky. We were mutually attracted at our first meeting, and remained close companions for several years. This, of course, led me to feel at home, no longer a stranger in a foreign land.

Life seemed on an even keel. I was able to conduct my business interests increasingly by internet communication with short monthly trips to London for actual face-to-face meetings. Jelena enjoyed these trips, too, quickly fitting into the rather different British tradition and culture.

I learned that as a Russian, she was proud to be Estonian and had worked hard to achieve the full Estonian and new EU passports.

Looking back on my experiences in Estonia, I realise how fortunate I was to make several close friends. Ander and Hannah Ild were my first Estonian friends, providing endless insights into daily life in that rapidly developing, newly independent country. Perhaps above all, their love of their native culture, especially its architecture and manorial heritage. Indeed, the almost fully restored Neeruti manorand park is a testimony to their dedication to their heritage. Imagine taking a complete wreck of a huge house and having the imagination and resolution to restore it to its former glory!

Sadly, Vladimir Volohhonski died prematurely, suffering a long and distressing illness and leaving a desolate family, including Alex, his eldest son. Alex's first words to me—that there are two Estonias, Russian Estonia and Estonia—were born out in my own experiences over the years. Of course, there is the negative side as evidenced by the tragic monument crisis, but there is also a positive side. On the one hand, patriotism, pride in one's own culture and country, is a great virtue as long as it does not descend into narrow nationalism. And on the other hand, respect for other cultures is essential in any civilisation. I think the majority of those living in Estonia today have learned something from the lessons of the past and are prepared to live in peace and harmony with each other.

Living abroad is also enhanced by having the companionship of compatriots, in my case, Fred Bristol,

Toby Stone, and Steve Metcalfe. We largely led our separate lives, but it was good to know they were around, and it was fun to meet up over a good dinner and compare notes.

7

RUSSIAN ENTERPRISE, PART 2

Russian Railways

Having gained confidence through the experience and success of DSL Alpha, I was on the lookout for other enterprising opportunities which usually appeared unexpectedly over the years.

I first encountered Vladimir Yakunin[37] at the Rhodes Forum, held each autumn on that lovely and historic island. The forum provides a platform for serious discussion about contemporary cultural, political, and religious challenges. It attracts a large number of significant leaders and individuals from all over the world. For instance, I met and had a lengthy conversation with the head of the Confucianist Order of China. Thankfully, his English was excellent, and

---

[37] Vladimir Yakunin b. 30 June 1948. President, Russian Railways June 2005 to August 2015. Author of *The Treacherous Path—An insider's Account of Modern Russia*, 2018.

Eastern Encounters

I learned of the largely unreported—in the West anyway—revival of Confucianism within communist China today. It is a sign of China slowly rediscovering its ancient roots.

The Rhodes Forum was the brainchild of Vladimir Yakunin, whose presence cast an uplifting spell on the proceedings. It also became clear that his vision impacted not only the forum but his business and charitable activities in Russia. He was originally one of the inner circle of influential people in St Petersburg who encouraged Vladimir Putin to enter the political game and who supported him in achieving the Russian success story of today. Hence, Yakunin ultimately found himself president of Russian Railways, the largest employer in the Russian Federation. His success in that role was phenomenal, creating a railway structure the envy of the world and which includes its own hospitals, schools, and amazing employee facilities. When I was first in Russia in 1991, the railway journey from St Petersburg was twelve hours. My most recent trip recently was just under four hours in a first-class train. In fact, so impressed I was that I telephoned Vladimir to tell him I was enjoying his famous train and looked forward to seeing him in Moscow. To my surprise, he said, "Sadly not, as I am in the Dorchester in London."

17. With Vladimir Yakunin, president, Russian Railways, Tallinn, 2013.

One weekend in 2011 I was invited to a gathering in Vienna presided over by Vladimir Yakunin. Many interesting people had gathered, revealing the extent of his connections. For example, this time I met and conversed with the famous Abbot Ephraim of Vatopedi Monastery on Mount Athos, where the Prince of Wales often stayed and which I was to be privileged to visit a few years later.

During the weekend, my friend Father Anton Illin told me that Vladimir Yakunin had a serious challenge. It was to establish an appropriate contact in Abu Dhabi to explore the opportunity for a joint venture with Union Rail, later known as Etihad Rail.

I had recently met, through Nick Stalder Elena Chiotis, who had been close to the Abu Dhabi ruling family since the days of the founding ruler Sheikh Zayed.[38] I decided to ring Elena, and she immediately said she could arrange a meeting for Vladimir Yakunin with Sheikh Mohammed bin Khalin Al Hamed, who would gladly assist. I was hastily invited to a meeting with Yakunin and his entourage. He was so enthusiastic to meet Sheikh Mohammed that he said he would postpone his holiday to attend. Not only did this occur, but also unusually, the sheikh agreed to the meeting despite it being during Ramadan.

On 9 August 2011, Vladimir Yakunin, accompanied by Russian Railways vice president Alexander Sultanov,[39] arrived in Abu Dhabi in the presidential jet. Greeting him, Yakunin turned off his mobile, ending a call with President Putin, who was wishing him well for the meeting. We drove straight to Sheikh Mohammad's office, and after a short but tense meeting, a memorandum of understanding was signed. Though this led to a series of further meetings, including one in Moscow, no actual business was forthcoming, a great disappointment to us all. However, goodwill was

---

[38] Sheikh Zayed bin Sultan Al Nahyan.
[39] Russian deputy foreign minister, 2007.

engendered, eventually leading to an interesting event at the House of Lords.

17. With HH Sheikh Mohammad bin Khalid al Hamid and Vladimir Yakunin, Abu Dhabi, 2011.

As chairman of the UK Guild of Travel and Tourism, I had come to see that there was a growing opportunity for tourism in Russia. This was also understood at Russian Railways, who was developing luxury train journeys throughout the Russian Federation and beyond. Most famous are the Golden Eagle Luxury Trains which were just being introduced. Thus, I suggested to Vladimir that we should hold a celebratory lunch at the House of Lords with him as guest speaker.[40] He

---

[40] Held on 14 March 2012.

brought with him a distinguished Russian delegation, and we gathered a cross-section of the "great and the good"—members of the Houses of Lords and Commons; editors; travel tycoons; and not forgetting Princess Katarina, president of the Guild. I learned for the first time during that event that Vladimir was born and brought up in Tallinn before the family moved to St Petersburg. Then I understood his generosity to Estonian causes, especially his generous assistance in covering most of the costs of the new Russian Church in Lasnamae, Tallinn. A few years later, we were to stand together at the first liturgy performed in the church presided over by Patriarch Kirill.[41]

On the day Vladimir was sanctioned by the Americans, I called him in solidarity. He said, "Thank you for your understanding, but luckily, I have no money in the USA, and I am just joking about this with President Putin, who sends his best regards!"

He retired as president of Russian Railways in 2015. Soon afterwards, I was staying at the Astoria Hotel and on impulse rang him. "Amazing timing", he said. "I have just arrived in St Petersburg for one night before going to Moscow." I invited him to join me for breakfast and was delighted he was free to do so as I needed his advice about a secret issue.

He also told me that he was planning an

---

[41] Patriarch of Moscow and all Rus. B. 20 November 1946. Elected Patriarch 1 February 2009.

autobiography—*The Treacherous Path: An Insider's Account of Modern Russia*—which was published in 2018. This is a must for any serious understanding of contemporary Russia by one of its creators.

The North Caucasus

It is very sad when a worthy project fails. The Home Group was the brainchild of Sasha Filatov, who gave his all for the implementation of the magnificent vision of a master plan for redevelopment of the North Caucasus. When such projects gain huge publicity at an early stage, jealousies and rivalries often result. This was, unfortunately, the case with the Home Group, landing poor Sasha in the notorious Batyrka Prison for, as he said, "To prevent me from working, limit my freedom and activity."

My friend Anton Ilin, doctor, priest, and visionary, first introduced me to Sasha, and based on such a high recommendation, I gladly met him for a preliminary discussion at the headquarters of Fund Sport in Moscow. Whilst waiting for Sasha to appear, I noticed some graffiti on the wall—a series of scrawled signatures, including Vladimir Putin's! *A good omen*, I thought. Sasha later explained that the room had been an election headquarters in earlier times.

Stimulated by Sasha's vision, I discussed the project with several of my British friends, who all agreed this

Eastern Encounters

was worth looking into further. So in December 2011, a general meeting was held at the headquarters of Fund Sport. As well as Sasha and me, the group included Yuri Kuznetsov and his daughter Sonia, acting as translator. Eric Nagal and Dirk Bergader, partners of Collineo,[42] our potential investment partners, and Nicholas Stalder were also there. It was unanimously agreed to set out a detailed business plan. A second meeting of the above participants, plus Hans-Wegner Hartmaan, our legal adviser, took place in early January 2012.

By now it was becoming clear that Sasha's plan needed to be presented in distinctive parts with the initial emphasis on a sport and tourist complex in Sochi, aptly named Olympic Home, and the construction of a highway linking Minerainge Vody, Elbrus, and Skhumi through the Baksan gorge and Kluhorsky pass.

It should be understood that the eyes of the sporting world were beginning to focus on the Western Caucasus, Sochi in particular, where the 2014 Winter Olympics were to be held. Hence our name, Olympic Home.

---

[42] Collineo Group GMBH, specialists in investing early in large development projects.

18. At Olympic Village, Sochi, 2014.

With such a huge challenge, it was decided to establish a London office, so a UK company, Regal Recreation and Resorts, was established as part of what was now becoming known as the Home Group.

By June 2012, both the Moscow and London offices were hives of activity, with London's main preoccupation being both public relations for the project and searching out potential investors in case any problems developed with Collineo.

Steve Metcalfe headed up the London team, that

by now included Fred Bristol, Simon Reading,[43] and Christopher Mackenzie Beevor.[44] None of us had been to the Caucasus region, and we realised that if we were to be convincing, this should be quickly remedied.

Thus, in mid-June, the highly excited team set off from Moscow under the direction of Sasha, who had led numerous delegations to the region and had developed friendships with many key players. Time being of the essence, it was decided to concentrate on just two key areas, Karachaevo—Circassia and Kabardino—Balkaria. We landed in Mineralnye Vody and were driven to the capital, Cherkessk, where we were received most graciously by Rashid Temrezov, head of the People's Assembly.

Only in 1926, did Cherkessk receive its name. It was formerly known as Bata Ipashinsk by a decree of Tsar Alexander II. Ultimately it became the capital of Karachaevo, Circassia. During World War II, the city was occupied by the Germans experiencing some heavy fighting and many casualties. Thus, it was appropriate that we were first taken to the dramatic monument to the Soviet soldiers of Cherkessk in the city centre.

Next we were taken to the Hall of Government, where Rashid Temrezov led us into the impressive Council Chamber. There we were seated to receive President Temrezov's speech of welcome and introduction of

---

[43] Simon Charles Henry Rufus Isaacs, fourth marquess of Reading.
[44] Colonel Christopher David, Mackenzie Beevor CBE.

the cabinet ministers. Sasha Filatov was invited to address the gathering, introducing the members of our delegation and explaining the aims of project Elbrus, emphasising that the key to the development of any territory is the transport infrastructure, hence our vision of the arterial highway. Sasha's speech was well received—applause all round—and was enthusiastically endorsed by the president.

19. The Regal Recreations and Resorts team with the president of Karachaevo-Cherkeisia, 2012.

After a lavish reception and group photo on the parliament steps, we set forth on our journey to Kabardino-Balkaria. Thankfully, the June days are long in the region, allowing us plenty of time to absorb the majestic landscape of mountains, hills, valleys, and rivers over which we crossed via ancient, narrow stone bridges. So impressive was the journey that silence reigned over us. Even me! Occasionally we stopped to take in the landscape which seemed to be deserted apart from occasional goats and sheep. At our last stop, we gazed across a valley towards a large derelict building, a remnant of Soviet times.

20. Soviet monument on the road to Cherkessk, Colonel Christopher Mackenzie-Beevor CBE, the Marquess of Bristol, and Fr Dr Anton Ilin.

It was dusk as we arrived in Nalchik, the capital of Kabardino-Balkaria, but light enough to see the splendid presidential palace where we were guests of President Arsen Kanokov.[45]

And it was a night to be remembered. Some fifty or so guests had been assembled by President Kanokov to meet and greet this distinguished British delegation! After generous drinks and mixing with local dignitaries, we were bidden to an exotic banquet of exquisite local delicacies served by equally exotic waitresses. Sasha and I were privileged to be seated on either side of our host, though not in the Western way but crossed legs on sumptuous cushions. We lounged in splendid comfort. Local musicians played as dancers and singers performed.

21. Oriental banquet with the President of Kabardino-Balkaria, 2012.

---

[45] Head of the Kabardino-Balkar Republic from 2005 to 2013.

During our conversation, when the entertainment permitted, the president suggested that the next day we might like to ascend Mount Elbrus. Of course, we were completely in the hands of Sasha, who, with I thought a twinkle in his eyes, enthusiastically agreed. We knew about Elbrus from our project discussions but had not taken in that it is the highest and most prominent peak in Europe.[46] However, in the spirit of the intoxicating banquet, anything seemed possible, and I retired contentedly to bed in the early hours.

It was not easy rising at 07:30 after a few hours of deep sleep, but after a good breakfast, we were driven to the base of Elbrus. We were equipped with mountain—rather uncomfortable—boots, bright orange climber's wear, and dark goggles. The lower slopes of Elbrus are popular with skiers, and we began the ascent in a ski lift. After a half hour walk up a rough track, we came to a second ski lift, that takes more adventurous skiers to their highest feasible point. It was becoming chilly as we walked upwards, towards a couple huge snow tractors which were to take us to the halfway point. The higher we went, the more amazing the views became.

The lower part of the mountain had some forest which petered out into clumps of shrubs, wild and uncultivated, amidst towering rocks and smaller boulders. Then suddenly, they all disappeared under

---

[46] It stands 5,642 metres above sea level.

Michael Wynne-Parker

snow, endless snow. As though to cheer us, Sasha told of human skeletons occasionally appearing in the windswept snow. Some of the skeletons supposedly remained from the Second World War which raged in the region, and the others of more recent climbing victims. Every year the mountain claims about thirty lives. We became less complacent about our ascent despite the reasonable comfort of the snow tractors.

After an hour or so, we were invited to leave the tractors and began a slow march upwards in single file. The air was becoming distinctly thinner, and sunshine had replaced the former gloomy conditions. We were glad for our dark goggles. Soon we saw another snow tractor which would take us towards our destination. And an amazing vehicle it was! It bounded over rocky terrain and then suddenly crawled at quite a pace up what seemed to be sheer rock. Now I was clinging on to the tractor's side and understood the importance of the heavy seat belt. At one point, Fred Bristol asked me if I had any heart pains. I, being much older, replied thankfully not. Someone commented, "Nothing to worry about. Anton[47] is here, and if you are sick, he is a doctor. And if you die, he is a priest. So nothing to worry about."

We finally disembarked and again, but now more slowly, walked single file to the summit. I was feeling

---

[47] Father Dr Anton Ilin.

light-headed and a little breathless. I was thankful when we were told we had arrived. Out came a hip flask or two in celebration. We stood in awe at the staggering views in all directions. It was indeed amazing to realise that on our side and below, we were in Russia. And just below on the other side was Georgia.

Thankfully, someone had thought to bring a camera and took a picture, proof that we really were there! Mobile phones ceased to work as we reached a certain height, hence the importance of the camera.

I think we were all rather relieved to be back in the snow tractor to make our hazardous descent and completely relieved to actually arrive safely back at base. There was quite a reception committee awaiting us, including some journalists, all interested to meet this group of British adventurers! Said one to me, "How did it compare with Mt Everest?"

I needed to disappear inside the local facility. I was shocked when I looked in a mirror and saw my face was blood-red. Later, a doctor in London told me we had taken an irresponsible risk without using portable oxygen apparatus. Thankfully, I didn't know of the risk at the time. After all, as the saying goes, "Nothing ventured, nothing gained."

The experience of Mt Elbrus was, at least to me, the highlight of our Caucasian adventure, despite the ultimate failure of the Home Group project.

22. At the ascent of Mt Elbrus, 2012.

That night we stayed in a delightful small hotel at the foot of the mountain. After a celebratory dinner, it was sheer joy to sink into a deep sleep.

The next day we explored more of the Elbrus region before leaving Nalchik, aware of growing media interest in our project. But we remained unaware that a rival group was taking a deep interest in our activities. It was, however, a real blow to hear of Sasha's arrest and consequent imprisonment. I remember the day well. Prince Michael had been supportive of our London efforts towards the success of the project and had agreed to visit the Moscow headquarters on 9 October 2012. I received an urgent phone call early that morning from Sonia Kuznetsov to say that police had entered the headquarters! Thankfully, I was able to get Igor Lapshin on the phone, and he at once agreed to meet Prince Michael at the hotel and inform him, "Change of plan, sir." So Prince Michael enjoyed a cultural tour instead of meeting the Moscow police.

It quickly became clear to us all that very sadly we would have to abandon the Home Group project. Sasha was imprisoned on false charges and paid the price not only of extreme discomfort for a year but also, perhaps worse, of seeing his magnificent dream shattered.

8

RUSSIAN CULTURE, PART 2

The year 2014 started on an optimistic note as far as Anglo-Russian cultural cooperation was concerned. A great banquet was held in The Cavalry and Guards Club to which the great and the good of both nations came, including Prince Michael, Russian ambassador Alexander Yakovenko, Archbishop Elisey, Vasily Shestakov, Michael Binyan of *The Times*, the Marquess of Bristol, Major General Walter Courage, Princess Katya Galitzine, Princess Katarina, Lady Olga Maitland, Prince Dimitri Lobanov-Rostovski, Princess Selene Obolensky, Ian Paisley MP, the Marquess of Reading, General Sir David Richards, and Count Nikolai Tolstoy. Colonel Christopher Mackenzie-Beevor welcomed all and proclaimed great days ahead for cultural cooperation. Little could we know that by the middle of the year, UK-Russian relations would begin to gradually decline.

Also present at the banquet was Anatoly Khopetskiy.

Eastern Encounters

He had written a novel about Russian orphan Vasily Oschshepkov and how he found himself in Tokyo about 1904, where he learnt Kadokan Judo, from which he went on to develop SAMBO.

23. With Anatoly Khlopetskiy and Princess Selene Obolensky at the inaugural dinner of the Anglo-Russian Cultural Exchange, 27 January 2014.

24. With Vassily Shestakov at the Anglo-Russian Dinner, 2014.

SAMBO

One evening in early 2012, I was invited by Simon Reading to attend a reception in honour of SAMBO. Initially I was confused as long ago this was a name used to call station porters to one's aid ! It was quickly explained by Simon that Sambo is a combination of martials arts very close to traditional judo. I later understood it to be an acronym for Samooborona Bez Oruzhiya.[48] Having early training in judo, I at once became interested and eagerly attended the reception,

---

[48] Literally translates as, "Self defence without weapons."

Eastern Encounters

where I was to meet Vasily Shestakov, president of the International SAMBO Federation. His knowledge and enthusiasm gripped my imagination, and I decided to explore further. I discovered that the sport is relatively modern since its development began in the early 1920s as the Soviet army improved its hand-to-hand combat capabilities. It had developed into a merger of the most effective martial arts techniques including Japanese judo, Armenian Kokh, Georgian Chidaoba, Romanian Trinta, Uzbek Kurash, Mongolian Khapsagay, Pakistani Pahlavi, Indian Kushta, Nigerian Igba, and here at home most amazingly Cornish and Westmorland wrestling! All of them can recognise their traditions and heritage in SAMBO. Thus, it is a unique sport of truly international origin and international character. I also learned from Vasily that after a great deal of negotiations, SAMBO was likely to be recognised by the International Olympic Committee. All very exciting, and I at once decided to get involved. Not only because of my personal interest in sport, but also because I realise that sport, culture, and often business do more to bridge international divisions than politics.

Vasily was to become a regular visitor to London over the next few years. We became good friends not only in the United Kingdom but also in Russia.

In June 2013, two important events marked Vasily's second London visit. Firstly, he received the Freedom of the City of London, an ancient honour allowing the recipient, amongst other things, to drive a flock of sheep over London Bridge. Vasily was told that he was the first Russian to receive the honour since the days of the old Muscovy Company in 1645.

Secondly, the main reason for Vasily's visit was to attend a gala dinner at Kensington Palace. This was a great achievement and a sign that SAMBO was gradually being given the recognition it deserved. Indeed, the sport was rapidly spreading throughout the British Commonwealth, leading to the establishment of the Commonwealth SAMBO Association of which Simon Reading became its first president. Indeed, it was greatly due to his energy and influence that a distinguished gathering attended this impressive event. The evening began with a SAMBO demonstration on the palace lawn, somewhat to the surprise of passers-by. Inside we went to a splendid champagne reception followed by a sumptuous dinner. I was honoured to be a speaker, and it was subsequently announced that I was to become chairman of the Commonwealth SAMBO Association under Lord Reading. A rapid rise indeed!

Almost immediately I received an invitation to attend the SAMBO World Championships in St Petersburg, along with Simon Reading and Leo Malin, a highly enthusiastic supporter. It was an awe-inspiring event attended by President Putin. Whether or not Simon had whispered into the president's ear that I was celebrating my birthday, I was surprised to be told that a birthday treat lay in store. Leo and I were whisked off to a very special banyan. It was not my first experience with this exhilarating treatment, but it was for Leo, who let out several moans as fierce heat rose within the first treatment chamber. On the principle that heat rises, I had chosen the lowest deck, whilst Leo had leapt to the top one. Freezing water followed in the pool we had to cross before entering the second chamber consisting of birch floggings and other blood-stimulating experiences. The treatments continued for two hours, certainly my longest, and we were in high spirits and very hungry as we enjoyed my birthday dinner.

This was Leo's first visit to St Petersburg, and we had an enjoyable few hours the next day in The Hermitage.

Andrew Moshanov must be given full credit for introducing SAMBO into many Commonwealth countries, and we felt ready to embark on a first Commonwealth championships to be known thereafter as the President's Cup. After a huge amount of planning, the event was scheduled for 27 September 2014, and held at the Bluewater Glow, London. It was a spectacular event attracting about 1,500 spectators.

Originally the event was to be staged at the Old Bishops Gate in the centre of London. But after much deliberation, the organising committee felt to attract a large audience it was better to find a venue which was more attractive and easier to reach. Andrew Moshanov's suggestion of the Glow in Dartford was thought ideal. The Glow is part of the Bluewater Shopping Centre, easy to reach by motorway, and has free parking.

The event had two mats, and the competition was divided into two sections. Division 1 teams were Russia, Azerbaijan, Belorussia, and Kazakhstan. Division 2/3 Team Great Britain—Team GB–with Commonwealth Africa, Commonwealth America, and Commonwealth Asia-Oceania. The top mat was designated for the Division 1 teams. These were the showpiece teams here to impress, and they certainly did. But it was the Division 3 teams that created the most interest with a very patriotic audience waving their Union flags. The group was very evenly matched, with all of them wanting to reach the finals against the Division 1 winner.

Team GB's first match was against the united team of Commonwealth Africa, and what a start! There were wins for Bradley Belsey, Casey Belsey, Ashley Costa, Kerrie Penfold, Danny Carritt, Danny Roberts, Barry Gibson, and Karl Etherington. So eight wins for Great Britain, giving them a standing ovation. What a result!

Next was Team GB versus the united team of Commonwealth America with seven wins for Team GB. This group produced one of the devastating throws of the tournament. Ashley Costa had won many British titles in SAMBO, Kurash, and judo, and this was his last tournament as he was to retire after the event. His favourite technique was a pickup, so it was ironic

Eastern Encounters

that he was caught with his own throw and rendered unconscious. I am glad to say he recovered very quickly.

So the GB team achieved what it set out to do and made the final with Russia. Team Russia, which had been competing with Kazakhstan, Belarus, and Azerbaijan, had impressed the audiences and VIPs alike. As expected, the GB team lost 7 to 2, but I to be honest, our two wins were really because the Russian players withdrew because of injury. Yet Team GB fought its hearts out, and the British SAMBO Federation was very proud of its team. The whole event was a tremendous success, and it was unanimously decided to make the President's Cup an annual event. President Shestakov was clearly impressed and kindly wrote as follows:

> Dear Mr Wynne-Parker,
> On behalf of the international SAMBO Federation (FIAS) and in my personal capacity let me congratulate you on a successful running of the 2014 SAMBO President's Cup in London. Due to you personally and your qualified colleagues the competitions were held at the highest level. The commitment and diligence that were shown during the preparation to the competitions distinctly reflect your serious and scrupulous attitude towards our

common cause which is the development of SAMBO worldwide.

We highly appreciate the current relations and hope for the further fruitful and productive cooperation for the sake of SAMBO development.

Let me also wish you and the Commonwealth SAMBO Association success and prosperity.

We are pretty confident that our joint efforts in SAMBO development will lead us to the desired purpose which is inclusion of SAMBO into the Olympic Programme.

Best Regards,

FIAS President Vasily Shestakov

Consequently, the following September, the event was arranged in Manchester and attended by the mayor, Tony Lloyd. It coincided with Manchester United versus Sunderland at the famous Old Trafford Stadium, where the mayor had kindly arranged a box for us. It was a fantastic experience to see Manchester United win 3–0. During the event, I was informed that Simon Reading was resigning as president of the Commonwealth

SAMBO Association, and shortly afterwards, I was honoured to be appointed his successor.

My first engagement as president was to attend the Seventh International Scientific Congress's "Sport, People and Health" held in St Petersburg, 27–29 October, where I was challenged to make a presentation on psychosomatic aspects of sport from my personal experiences. Thankfully, it seemed to be received well!

The third President's Cup was held in Edinburgh 2016 and was attended by Scottish sports legend Maurice Allen, who agreed to make an instructive commentary throughout. For the next three years, the President's Cup was held again in London and twice in Northern Ireland, where Ian Paisley[49] warmly welcomed us into his famous constituency.

On 26 April 2016, Vasily Shestakov invited me to participate in an event in the State Duma, Moscow, an exhibition opening celebrating the Russian-British sport association. By this time a political chill had influenced UK-Russian relations, and for not the first time, I was the only British representative at this significant event. I was delighted to address the gathering on the importance of sport as a unifying factor. The comments were taken up by state media, including a headline on the six o'clock news. This led to an interesting meeting the next morning. More on that later.

---

[49] Ian Paisley, MP for North Antrim, Northern Ireland.

In 2018, it was with great interest that I attended the SAMBO World Championships in Sochi. Based on previous visits, I was ready to expect huge transformations due to the Winter Olympics. But I was not prepared for the sheer scale and magnitude of the stadium, its immediate environment, and the whole regional infrastructure. I made sure to take time out from the official event to view the magnificent ski resorts, hotels, and numerous cultural facilities. The World Championships are always impressive, but this one was magnificent not only because of the growing international participation but, of course, because of the setting.

One of my greatest joys and honours was to participate in Vasily Shestakov's sixty-fifth birthday celebrations on 4 April 2018.

It was a splendid occasion in Moscow's Four Seasons hotel. All the great and the good of Moscow were present, and I was privileged indeed to prepare the midnight toast to Vasily's health, wealth, and happiness. During the early part of the proceedings, I developed a husky voice and by the end of dinner, could hardly utter. A great relief, I suppose, to some. I confided to my dinner companions that I was in urgent need of honey and whiskey (as a cure). Amazingly, it was pointed out that every guest had a gift bag which included a pot of honey! It didn't take long for the Four Seasons to find a fine Scotch whisky, and by five to midnight, I was in fine form. I spoke in English, and Alexander Korsik brilliantly interpreted, though I could see many assembled understood English perfectly. The toast ended by my singing 'Many Years' in ancient Slavonic which raised a loud round of applause. Whether for my speech or singing, I am not sure. My adrenaline was clearly surging as I escorted Vasily's wife, Tatiana, round the dance floor—followed by so many other grand Moscow ladies that I hardly remember falling into bed in the early hours.

Imperial Orthodox Palestine Society

For those of monotheistic descent, of faith, Jerusalem is the centre of the world. Surely, therefore, it ought to be the historic unifying factor between these three religions. But sadly, the opposite is true. Today the Israeli-Palestinian conflict graphically illustrates my point, and sadly, the Christians are largely silent.

As a young man, I was thrilled to be invited to Jerusalem for the second time by Father Anthony Grabbe[50] in 1971. As described in my book *If My Table Could Talk*,[51] I met Father Anthony in New York in 1966, and consequently, he invited me to join him in the Holy City. It was during this visit that I first experienced the activities of the Imperial Orthodox

---

[50] Father Anthony Grabbe (Count Alexei Georgievich Grabbe), 1971.
[51] *If My Table Could Talk*, published 2011.

Palestine Society (IOPS). So as to cause no offence to my Jewish friends, I should explain that the society was so named by its founder, Grand Duchess Elizabeth[52], in 1882, when the area of the Holy Land was universally known as Palestine. The state of Israel only came into existence in 1948.

It was Father Anthony who first pinned the badge of the IOPS on my lapel and declared me a member.

The original aim of the IOPS was to raise funds to enable Russians to make their pilgrimage to the holy sites. Pilgrimage has been a central activity of religion from earliest times, and it was obvious that the majority of Russian Orthodox believers could not possibly afford such an experience. Grand Duchess Elizabeth, encouraged by her brother-in-law Alexander III, enthusiastically set about fundraising. Here is an example of her international appeal:

> To his Eminence Platon,
>   Archbishop of the Aleutian Isles and North America
>
> Your Eminence,
>   I impose upon myself the especially pleasant duty of expressing to Your Eminence My cordial gratitude for the very successful collection conducted in the

---

[52] Grand Duchess Elizabeth Feodorovna, 1864–1918.

churches under your jurisdiction on the Palm Sunday of the past 1910 year. This collection was taken for the needs of the Imperial Orthodox Palestinian Society of which I am a president.

The hearty response and sympathy with which you, Vladyko, always relate to our Orthodox Russian cause in the Holy Land, energetically and fruitfully realized by the Palestinian Society, gives me assurance that in the new 1911 year Your Eminence will also make the necessary order to take a collection for the satisfaction of the urgent needs of Orthodoxy in the Holy Land on the coming Palm Sunday in the churches under your jurisdiction.

The appeals needed for the collection, sign-up sheets and receipts are enclosed.

I am entrusting myself to your hierarchical prayers.

Sincerely disposed towards you,
Elizabeth
18 January 1911

Interestingly, some support came from the United Kingdom. Elizabeth was a favoured niece of Queen Victoria, whose respect for her somewhat overcame her doubts about the Russian Orthodox religion.

Incidentally, we often forget how important the royal families of Britain, Russia, and Germany were in keeping the fragile peace before the First World War.

So successful was the fundraising that hundreds of thousands of pilgrims visited the Holy Land between 1882 and 1912, and the IOPS became not only prosperous but also extremely influential.

In Jerusalem I became aware of the large number of churches, monasteries, and hospices which the society had established, all bearing the society's emblem on their doorways.

In Russia, partly because of imperial support, the society became the principal cultural society with an impressive headquarters and museum in Moscow. In London, the grand duchess was honoured by a statue over the main door of Westminster Abbey.

As the years passed, I became increasingly aware of both the historical and cultural significance of the IOPS. However, I never anticipated playing a significant role until 5 June 2012, when I found myself addressing a large gathering of its members in Moscow.

I had become aware that the IOPS had been revived by Sergei Stepashin under the blessing of Patriarch Kiril. Together with Sergei Mannik and Alexander Volohhonski, I attended the gathering in the Manezh Expo Centre, next to the Kremlin, and at the appointed time rose to speak. It was realised at once that many present had little understanding of English, so for the first time in his life, poor Alex had to act as interpreter. He rose to the occasion with distinction which only encouraged me to enter enthusiastically into my subject.

It was obvious that most present were amazed that here was an Englishman who had witnessed historical events in the society during the period when it was relegated to a 'scientific body' in Russia during the Soviet period. I think they were amazed to hear how Father Anthony Grabbe had almost single-handedly successfully sued the Israeli government over illegal occupation of IOPS property and was awarded $1m in the 1970s.

Following my Moscow speech, I was asked to be a founder-trustee of the Estonian branch of the IOPS by Sergei Mannik, the founder. I happily served alongside Alex, who had also become a trustee. Representing the Estonian branch, I attended the Annual IOPS Conference on Friday, 2 June 2017, in Moscow, held in the Cathedral of Christ the Saviour Conference Centre. It was there that I had the privilege of a first encounter with Sergei Stepashin.

The introduction was made by Igor Lapshin at the end of the conference. Sergei Stepashin has had a long and prominent role in Russia, including a brief period as prime minister in 1999, before which he held the posts of minister of international affairs and minister of justice, as well as director of the Federal Security Service. It is entirely due to Sergei Stepashin's enthusiasm that the

IOPS, of which he was appointed head in 2007, has grown from strength not only in Russia but increasingly throughout Europe and beyond.

My encounter was brief but allowed for a mutually favourable impression. Within a few weeks, I was invited to head the first branch of the IOPS in the United Kingdom. I received written confirmation of this from Daniel Burduga on 28 July.

To operate successfully in the United Kingdom, it became apparent that we should register the society with the charity commission. And after lengthy negotiations conducted with rigorous care by Simon Jennings, we were finally given registered status on 7 June 2019. This was the longest registration process I had ever encountered, and several of us had concluded that political considerations had probably come into play. Firstly, UK-Russian political relations were plunging into new depths, and secondly, the name Palestine is controversial to say the least! Patience is a virtue, and I have learned that determination usually wins the day.

The UK IOPS Society was launched at a formal dinner on 21 February 2019, attended by an impressive list of members and guests at the Cavalry and Guards Club. Greetings were conveyed from Sergei Shapashin by Igor Lapshin. A simple notice about the event on the *Daily Telegraph* court and social page attracted the attention of several journalists resulting in amazing headlines led by the *Sunday Times*, "Establishment flocks to dine at new society with Kremlin ties." Others followed: "The Kremlin high society banquet in Mayfair", *Daily Mail*, and it was even covered by the *Times* of Australia. Of course, the publicity caused quite a stir, and several commented that it was now clear that Mr Putin's influence ran right through British Society to the monarchy itself! Luckily, the British have a good sense of humour, and several chuckles were heard about the unlikely recruitment of patriotic generals and princesses becoming Russian spies!

26. Sergei Stepashin, Moscow IOPS HQ 2019, with Daniel Burduga, Elena Agapova, and Elena and Alex Chiotis.

27. Presenting IOPS documents from the 1970s to Sergei Stepashin, 2018.

Russkiy Mir Foundation

I first encountered the Russkiy Mir Foundation—or Russian World in plain English—through Father Anton Ilin of Mount Elbrus fame. He in turn introduced me to Vyacheslav Nikonov, head of the foundation since 2007. He is also the renowned grandson of Vyacheslav Molotov, the prominent Soviet foreign minister he was named after. He has had a very distinguished career as a Russian political scientist and currently a prominent member of the state duma. His several books include a biography of Molotov, more interesting than most because of their close relationship.

President Putin created the foundation to promote

Russian language and culture worldwide, and increasingly in cooperation with the Russian Orthodox Church, to promote traditional values which challenge the current Western ones. Hence the foundation takes an increasingly significant role in the present philosophical debate.

I have been privileged to attend several foundation events in Sochi and Moscow. But most memorable of all was the assembly in Suzdal in November 2015. Suzdal is part of the so-called Golden Ring cluster of ancient towns lying to the north and east of Moscow. There one becomes immediately aware of early Russian culture symbolised by the centuries-old Suzdal Kremlin, within which almost miraculously stands intact the thirteenth-century cathedral with its gold-starred domes and well-preserved frescoes. It is an architectural gem densely populated with eleven monasteries and twenty-five churches built between the twelfth and seventeenth centuries. No wonder it is a World Heritage site.

Some three hundred people attended the ninth Russkiy Mir Assembly. Most were from Russia, but quite a few of us came from various foreign parts. The theme was the eternal value of Russian literature.

The opening ceremony was held in the forum's hotel, Nikolaevsky Posad. Following the morning's proceedings, I was invited to join Vyacheslav Nikonov and his wife, Nina, for an enjoyable and instructive lunch. *This,* I thought, *is about as good as it gets!* No one could fail to be inspired by this dynamic man, whose historical, literary, and cultural knowledge is inspiring and whose enthusiasm is infectious. I thought that being part of this small luncheon group was more than enough to justify my assembly attendance! After an afternoon stroll round the ancient city, followed by a short siesta—having journeyed through the previous night—I braced myself for the evening session, during which I was to speak. My subject was England and the Rus: An Historical Perspective and Modern Challenge. I touched on the American led West's insensitivity to Russian history, the irresponsible stirring up of the rebels in the Maiden,[53] for example. I also spoke about the failure to appreciate the cultural and religious significance of Kiev, the first capital of the Rus, with its vital symbolism throughout evolving Russia. Well, the test for any speaker is the audience's response, and I was gratified with rigorous applause. Said one ageing Russian, "I am touched that there is at least one Englishman who really understands us!" Thankfully, there are many more.

Ruskiy Mir now has representation in many countries and understands that culture is one of the best ways of developing understanding and mutual cooperation.

---

[53] The Maiden Revolution took place in 2014, culminating in the ousting of President Viktor Yanukovych and overthrow of the Ukrainian government.

M.ART Foundation

As previously mentioned, the 26 April 2016, address at the opening of an exhibition celebrating Russian British Sport was reported on the main six o'clock news. Later that evening, I received a phone call from Roman Prokopiev, inviting me to meet him at the headquarters of the M.ART Foundation in Tverskaya-Yamskaya Street. I had heard previously about this dynamic and well-connected young man and of his entrepreneurial skills, so I was keen to meet him.

Having been warmly welcomed, I was asked if I minded having my portrait done by none other than famous portrait painter Georgy Shishkin.[54] Naturally I did not object. It was a strange sensation both engaging in an interesting conversation whilst being the subject of a portrait! Becoming absorbed in our discussion, however, I quickly forgot the famous artist.

Roman told me of the exciting plans he had for the M.ART Foundation, and to my surprise, he asked me if I would consider becoming a director to represent the United Kingdom. I said I was honoured to be considered, and within a few months, this was formalised.

After a couple hours, our meeting concluded, and I looked with astonishment at my completed portrait, in pastel, which Georgy had completed to perfection. Portraits can be controversial and often not to the

---
[54] Born 1948.

liking of the sitter, but in my case, I was happy. I told Roman and Georgy that my first portrait was done by Serge Rodzianko,[55] when I was twenty-eight. They were amazed to hear of Rodzianko's life in England and of his becoming a portrait artist in his late seventies.

Later, my portrait by Georgy was exhibited in an exhibition in the State Russian Museum (The Mikhailovsky Palace). Today it is part of the permanent M.ART Foundation Exhibition.

The M.ART Foundation today is a registered foundation and does much to foster a love of the arts as another way of contributing to understanding and communication.

It was through the M.ART Foundation that I was invited to visit the new Tretyakov Museum, where I was warmly received by the director, Zelfira Tregulova. It was a huge privilege to be escorted round gallery after gallery of amazing contemporary works of art from around the world.

Zelfira Tregulova was very well informed. She knew of my friendship with Ivan Lindsay,[56] who has one of the largest collections of soviet sculpture in the world. She paid great tribute to Lindsay, who had been astute enough to collect most of his sculptures in the early 1990s. I felt she hoped he might be prepared

---

[55] This story is told in my book *If My Table Could Talk*.
[56] Ivan Lindsay, author of Masterpieces of Soviet Painting and Sculpture

Eastern Encounters

to negotiate the return of some of the pieces to their homeland!

As we toured the museum, Zelfira showed me the view of the Cathedral of Christ the King close by and reminded me that just eighty-five years ago, the original cathedral had been blown up at Stalin's command from the very place we were standing.[57] Now, the newly rebuilt cathedral again dominates the landscape.

Ludvig Nobel Prize

If you mention the Nobel Prize, most people, at least in the West, think of Stockholm and the prize awarded each December to "Those who, during the preceding year, have conferred the greatest benefit to mankind."[58] It confers a stamp of approval on each recipient plus the magnificent sum of 10 million SEK (approximately £1million). The first award was given in 1901.

What is not so well known is that Ludvig Immanuel Nobel was of Swedish-Russian descent, and that the first Nobel Prize was awarded in Russia in 1896, to one Alexei Stepanov, for his treatise entitled "Fundamentals of Lamp Theory." The annual award, which continued until the 1917 Bolshevik intervention, was given under the auspices of the Nobel Brothers Production Association. The award was re-established in 2006

---

[57] 5 December 1931.
[58] Quote from Nobel, official documents.

Michael Wynne-Parker

by a group of like-minded people—Yaroslav Golko, who became chairman of the Honorary Council of the Ludvig Nobel Prize, and Anna Yakoleva and Evgeny Lukoshkov. Largely due to their efforts, Russia has restored this historic and prestigious tradition.

I had the privilege of meeting Anna Yakovleva and Evgeny Lukoshkov on one of my visits to St Petersburg in 2018. I remember it well. I had arrived a few days earlier at my favourite Astoria Hotel, next to St Isaac's famous cathedral, that had sadly become a museum during Soviet times, but now again has regular, well-attended services. The hotel was magnificently restored bySir Rocco Forte and his sister, Olga Polizzi, and within a ten-minute walk of Nevsky Prospekt and the Hermitage. So it has location, location, location[59] and is an oasis of comfort. Naturally, before my first visit to St Petersburg, I rang Sir Rocco who I had got to know through his brother-in-law, Robert Burness. He very kindly found the perfect suite with fine views of St Isaac's. One of the greatest pleasures after an absorbing day is to sit in the famous Litchfield Bar on the ground floor of the hotel, drinking with friends old and new. Everyone who is anyone in St Petersburg seems to be there!

Years before, I had experienced the amazing interiors created by Olga Polizziat Tresanton Hotel, Cornwall.

---

[59] *Location, Location, Location* is the title of a Channel 4 house-hunting TV show with Kirstie Allsopp and Phil Spencer.

It was she who had first told me of the St Petersburg Astoria plans. I always enjoyed finding her well-chosen selection of books to be found in every suite. And in the Astoria, they naturally included Tolstoy and Dostoyevsky.

It was a great joy to receive a call from Evgeny Lukoshkov inviting me to dinner, at which I learned something of the history of the Ludvig Nobel prizes' revival and present activities, including the annual award ceremony, held in the Constantine Palace and to which I was invited next afternoon.

It was a remarkable occasion. First the historic setting, the Constantine Palace, is usually known today as the National Congress Palace. It is a multifunctional complex including the state residence, a museum, and a modern congress venue. I and my friends had been asked to arrive earlier than the actual Nobel ceremony to be given a private tour of the state residence, the residence of President Putin when in St Petersburg. I will always remember climbing a narrow staircase to the president's observatory and being privileged to view the surrounding land and seascape through the telescope installed by Peter the Great.

Soon we were assembled in one of the palatial rooms appropriately decked out for the occasion. Trumpets sounded, the doors opened, and in came the official procession of Russian state guards, dignitaries, and the distinguished people who were to receive the award.

Each was formally introduced before being given the high honour. Thumbing through the beautifully produced programme, I saw familiar names of past recipients, including President Putin and Sergey Lavrov. Also listed was Prince Michael of Kent, who received the award for his dedication to UK-Russian relations. Clearly, the re-established award had acquired a new meaning, and the wide range of people who are awarded each year for their personal achievements has significantly expanded. I believe that one day, it will be as famous worldwide as the Swedish Nobel Prize is today.

Orthodox Russia

In my late teens, I attended my first Orthodox service in the Russian Church aptly named Emperor's Gate. I was the guest of the late Count Vladimir Kleinmichel, treasurer of the cathedral and who hosted a sumptuous lunch following the liturgy. Like Vladimir the Great's emissaries, I felt I was in heaven despite understanding very little of what was going on.

Looking back, this was my first lesson in what is the essence of Orthodoxy, that it is the heart and not the mind that perceives reality. I had gotten a glimpse of this in old-fashioned high Anglicanism but soon became disillusioned with the various shades of Protestantism and even brief encounters with Roman Catholicism.

Now clearly, there are many paths to truth in many religions, and millions of sincere believers who feel they are in the so-called right place. Having superficially researched some of them, I concluded that whatever one was engaged in better go to the source. And in Christianity, I thought, *Why not delve into the very first century?* Thus, I discovered the words of Eusebius and his account of the very earliest days of Christianity. I quickly became clear that Orthodoxy was the heir to the ancient faith in ritual, governance, and theology.

In 1966, as related in my book *If My Table Could Talk*, I met Father Anthony Grabbe[60] in New York, who almost immediately introduced me to his father, Bishop George Grabbe, in the Cathedral of Our Lady of the Sign, who marched me straight towards the altar, anointed me with holy oil, and pronounced me a member of the Russian Orthodox Church.

Soon afterwards, I went with Father Anthony to Jerusalem, where I witnessed the amazing Paschal fire[61] and became a member of the Imperial Orthodox Palestine Society, which I was to re-encounter many years later.

My very slowly evolving awareness of the spiritual impact of Orthodoxy lay only on the periphery of my life for many years. Indeed, until I had the privilege

---

[60] Cathedral of the Mother of God of the Sign, NY.
[61] The Paschal fire Easter vigil is described in detail on page 28 of my book *If My Table Could Talk*.

and joy of regularly attending St Alexander Nevsky Cathedral in Tallinn. There I learned my second lesson in Orthodoxy: Theology and academic instruction are not as important as immersion in the yearly cycle of liturgical practice.

As I have said, in Estonia I had the privilege of the influence of Metropolitan Cornelius, who attracted Orthodox personalities from various parts of the world and, of course, especially from Russia.

One such frequent visitor was Igor Lapshin. Igor has had a distinguished career in the Publishing Council of the Moscow Patriarchate, created in 1994, and involved in the coordination of various activities, including sourcing of specialist literary materials and organising exhibitions and overseas cultural activities. We also have a mutual friend in Alex Volohhonski and have enjoyed many occasions together in Moscow, Tallinn, and London—sometimes over a large cigar in deep philosophical discussion.

In early April 2011, Igor asked me if I would host a dinner in London for His Eminence Metropolitan Hilarion Alfeyev, the well-known head of external affairs of the Russian Orthodox Church. I happily agreed as I had devoured several of his literary works as well as been inspired by his musical compositions. His Eminence was in London for the launch of Patriarch Kirill's book *Freedom and Responsibility* at the London International Book Fair.

At 8 p.m., His Eminence Metropolitan appeared with his personal suite of clerics and Igor. To put them at ease, Igor explained in Russian, as several of them spoke little English, that dinner would proceed in traditional English form with toasts and speeches. As an Oxford graduate,[62] His Eminence well knew the etiquette and all present relaxed and entered into the spirit of the occasion. It was, of course, a huge honour for me to entertain so distinguished a guest. Little did I know then what remarkable events our meeting would lead to.

At about 10 p.m., His Eminence rose, and we all made for the club entrance, outside of which were three cars. As we parked, His Eminence gave me his blessing and added, "Let's be friends." This was a moving moment.

I returned inside, thinking to relax and absorb the events of the past two hours. But no sooner had I settled with a cigar and glass of port than five gentlemen appeared. They had cast aside their clericals and were determined to learn more of English club life. One of them was Father Anton Ilin, then permanent representative of the Russian Church at EU headquarters in Brussels. We begin a lifelong friendship that evening. Everyone enjoyed a long conversation late into the night as we hoped His Eminence was sleeping

---

[62] Pembroke College, Oxford, 1993–1995.

peacefully. He had just flown in from engagements in New York. It is amazing how after a couple of drinks even language barriers seem to disappear.

This happy evening led onto greater things. The following year, 2012, was the fifth anniversary of the reunion of the Russian Church, of the part which had continued in the West during the Soviet period and of the fully restored Mother Church of the Moscow Patriarchate. It was also the year of the fiftieth anniversary of the British Russian Orthodox Diocese of Sourozh.

Under the guidance of Archbishop Elisey, head of the Sourozh Diocese, plans were afoot to celebrate both events together in London. Sixteen bishops and archbishops, together with many others, gathered for a festive weekend that included a concert, conference, and festive luncheon at the Cavalry and Guards Club. During the luncheon on that warm summer's day,[63] when the windows were wide open, a large precession of protestors noisily passed below, causing one elderly Russian prelate to proclaim, "Is it the revolution?"

I met with Metropolitan Hilarion on several occasions in those days. At one luncheon he asked me if I had been on a pilgrimage to Mount Athos. When I answered, "Sadly not", to my surprise, he announced he was visiting the holy mount in a few days' time and

---

[63] 29 October 2012.

would like me to accompany him. This was an offer not to be refused, so I accepted at once. The next day I received all the necessary paperwork and detailed itinerary from the Metropolitan's secretary.

With great excitement, and not a little trepidation, I set out on 12 April 2013. The following is my diary account of the next few days.

> 12-4-2013
>
> Departed club at 5 a.m., taking BA flight to Thessaloniki. Was met by driver Leonides, who drove me to Makedonia Palace Hotel owned by Ivan Savidid, a Greek businessman born in Rostov-on-Don & a friend of Vladika, whose guest I am. This a very pleasant and newly developed hotel, & my room overlooks the sea. Able to unwind. Excellent luncheon followed by Cohiba (first cigar in 2 weeks!) & siesta (rather vital after 2 nights of approx. 4 hrs sleep). Met Father Anthony—assistant of the Metropolitan who is expected at 8:30 this evening. Discovered we must be away by 7 a.m.—so early to bed!
>
> 13/4 Downstairs at 7. Russian party led by the Metropolitan arrived at 7:20! Long but comfortable drive through increasingly remote & mountainous terrain & initial

mist giving way to brilliant sunlight as we ascended. Only incident—we were stopped by a mob who turned out to be 'green' demonstrators who relented at the sight of the Metropolitan & the diplomacy of Ivan Savidas, who travelled with us.

Finally arrived at small harbour—the arrival point for the new Thebaid Skete. A most fitting start to our pilgrimage. We climbed a long & steep path, passing buildings that had been in the midst of construction when the 1917/18 Revolution brought it to a sudden halt. Apparently there were about 400 monks here in 1917—almost all disappeared during the Communist regime. Now the Skete is being rebuilt with a skeleton number of monks, now 2 or 3. *Most* impressive situation & atmosphere. Birds singing. Wildflowers in abundance, butterflies—all this in mid-April. An ecological paradise. Even the seawater completely clear.

After a good look round, we descended the rugged pathway. (I was grateful to Vladika for his advice: "Take your walking shoes." Several of the Russian clergy stumbled in leather soles.) We embarked on two speedboats (at very high speed) to

St Pantelemons's Monastery—the R.O. Athos Mecca. Received by the Abbot, we proceeded into the main church to revere the relic of the Saint, after which into the refectory for a plain but tasty luncheon washed down by rather sweet tea.

Absolute peace!

After a brief rest, we set out in a convoy of 3 cars along primitive tracks. Sun high in a bright blue sky (glad I took Anton Z's advice bringing a light cap). Over the next 9 hrs we visited the following:

1) Old Rovssinon Skete undergoing restoration.
2) Xkenofan Monastery.
3) Xkenofan Mon. Icon, 40 Martyrs of Sebast, 10th Cent.

After this, Vladika H. headed back to Pantelemon Mon. to rest before all-night vigil/liturgy 8hrs! We continued in the expert hands of Ivan Savidis, who knows Mt A. intimately & is revered by the leadership for his generous support.

4) Visited the new & half constructed Church of St Nicodim (marble imported from India) & afterwards entertained by the priest-in-charge—very good local herbal tea.

Intoxicating local spirit & various Lenten foods & spectacular local oranges.

Luckily, we ate well as by the time we arrived back at St P., we had missed dinner. So truly fasted from about 8 to 7:30, when the liturgy was celebrated by V.. No electric lights. Showered by torchlight! Attended first 2 hrs of the vigil when received a message from Vladika to "go rest", & be up for the more important liturgy.

14th—After liturgy & breakfast (with red wine!) rested for an hour before setting off on the day's pilgrimage. Visited the following:

5) Iveron Monastery—The bells rang out as we arrived & went straight to see the famous Iveron icon of the Mother of God before Vladika performed the Akathist, after which we were shown the extensive collection of relics, inc. relics of St Peter & St Philip, 11th century. Good lunch.
6) Mylo Potamas cell, where lived St Athanasius, patriarch of Constantinople. Patriarch G lived in exile here in the early 20th cent. Had tea & liquors before a roaring log fire. Very atmospheric.

Eastern Encounters

7) Mylopotamas Skete and Vineyard—see book. Most impressive.
8) Kouloumousiou Mon., the venerated land of St Anna. Charming reception, tea ste.
9) Vatopedi, where greeted by old friend Abbot Ephraim. Prince Charles stayed here often, & I can understand why. Magnificent is an understatement. Veneration of the *belt of the Mother of God*. Then splendid dinner—calamari, salad, local wine—a feast. Then escorted to our rooms & free for 12 hours!

15th—Experienced the liturgy of the presanctified gifts in Greek before a sumptuous Lenten lunch followed by a long bumpy & @ times dangerous drive across the peninsular to:

10) St Paul's Mon., connected to Xkenofon Mon. and patronised by Tsar Nicholas? Here we venerated the gifts of the Magi.
11) St Dionysioos Mon. Ch. dedicated to St John the Baptist, whose relics are venerated.

We passed by boat St Gregory Mon. & the spectacular St Simon Peter <u>High Up</u>. Finally arrived 2 hrs late at the Capital Admin. Centre. Spent dinner & night with Father Joseph, who turned out to be a friend of Anthony Grabbe.

Mt Athos Impressions:

Majestic mysteries alluring. The Holy Mount rising out of a calm sea under a blue sky.

Stillness—Holy quiet—Beauty

Far from the madding crowd, strife, they pass the even tenor of their way.

Days free of *instant communication—*solitude

Ecological paradise. Nature in abundance.

Flowers (no pesticides) birds, butterflies, organic fruit & vegetables, exquisite wine from immaculately tended vineyards.

Warm welcome—smiling faces, gracious hospitality.

The monasteries, though constantly active in prayer, rituals, iconography, farming, and gardening, are calm and tranquil.

The monastic churches ornate & filled with ancient & impressive icons, remarkable relics, the air suffused by exotic incense (locally created). And harmonious voices intoning the mesmeric Greek chant.

The warm reception by much persecuted though most serene Abbot Ephraim.

Veneration of the holy relics of the Mother of God—her belt; St Anna, the gifts of the three wise men, St Peter, St Paul, St Philip. The holy icons and final supper with Father Joseph, who had remarkable links to my first Orthodox priest, Father Anthony Grabbe, & whose elder was his best friend! (Small world indeed.)

The leadership, friendship, & care of Vladyka Hilarion throughout the pilgrimage.

Michael Wynne-Parker

28. The fifth anniversary of the reunion of the Russian Church abroad and the Moscow Patriarchate, 20 October 2012.

29. St Pantelemon Monastery, Mt Athos, 2013.

Eastern Encounters

One memory stands out. During the visit to one of the monasteries, I noticed Metropolitan Hilarion standing alone, looking over a wall into the distance. I approached him, and something encouraged me to ask him what was his favourite book. "Of course", he said, "I must say the Bible. But otherwise, *Winnie the Pooh*."[64] This made quite an impression on me, and as soon as possible I reread the book I so enjoyed as a child. I began to understand something of its timeless wisdom.

Metropolitan Hilarion, in addition to his Episcopal duties, is well known as a composer. He once told me that he often 'heard' music during his walks along the River Thames whilst at Oxford, and I thought of the similarity with Mozart. Over the years, Metropolitan Hilarion's works have been performed many times throughout Europe, the United States, and Canada. He is one of Russia's most frequently heard composers. Therefore, it was with great pleasure that I agreed to be a sponsor of Vladyka's by now famous oratorio, "St Matthew Passion", on 8 February 2015, in London's Cadogan Hall. The event was organised superbly by Olga Balakleets, CEO and founder of Ensemble Productions, and it was performed by the Moscow Synodal Choir and the Russian Orchestra of London. Over a thousand people attended, including HRH Prince Michael of Kent and

---

[64] By A. A. Milne, 1926.

most appropriately, the Metropolitan's Principal Oxford tutor Kallistos Ware, now Metropolitan Kallistos.

30. With H. E. Metropolitan Hilarion Alfeyev before the performance of his oratorio "St Matthew Passion", Cadogan Hall, London, 2015.

Eastern Encounters

31. With Olga Balakleets, founder of Ensemble Productions, and HRH Prince Michael of Kent, Cadogan Hall, London, 2015.

Following the concert, we held a dinner for Metropolitan Hilarion at the Cavalry and Guards Club. I had asked him to invite anyone whoever he liked from the concert attendees and was delighted when he nominated Zamira Menuhin and her husband. It was a special joy for me as I had been honoured to meet her celebrated father, Yehdi Menuhin, many years before at the English-speaking Union Music Council.

It is probably largely due to the kind influence of Metropolitan Hilarion that I had the supreme honour of hosting the official banquet for His Holiness Patriarch Kirill of Moscow and all Russia during his visit to

London. I had been asked by Archbishop Elisey if I could possibly do this to save him from an awkward situation caused by several wealthy Russians vying with each other for the significant honour. The archbishop had consulted the Metropolitan, and somewhat to my surprise, I ended up as host! And on 16 October 2016, one hundred distinguished guests ascended the main staircase of the Cavalry and Guards Club to enjoy champagne and await the arrival of His Holiness.

Way back in July, Archbishop Elisey had been informed that Queen Elizabeth had graciously agreed to receive His Holiness at Buckingham Palace, and the patriarchal visit to London was based around that audience. It was seen by all who support UK-Russian friendship as highly significant. But sadly, it also attracted some opposition from anti-Russian media and the Ukrainian ambassador!

Of course, much effort went into the whole three-day event, but my efforts were solely focussed on the banquet, who to invite and who to leave out. The all-important menu—food and wines, flowers, table decorations, and the organisation of the reception at which all were to be introduced to His Holiness by appropriately chosen group leaders. And, of course, the all-important dinner seating plan.

All agreed the evening was a success, and I treasure the many letters of thanks received afterwards. Yes, some people still write proper letters in this digital age!

Picture the scene: One hundred seated at one long table with His Holiness in the centre. Dinner in candlelight, and harpist Maria Oakes playing tranquil background music. Conversation rising over good wines.

I was very conscious of my privilege as host to have His Holiness on my right, and I listened eagerly to his every wise word. Amazingly, we found that we have the same birthday. We spoke of gardening, one of his great interests, and of dogs. He spoke sadly of recently losing one of his, a Great Dane. Little did he know of a surprise awaiting him the next day, the gift of a Corgi puppy, the Queen's favourite breed. He was also amused to hear that the special chair upon which he was seated was the very one used by the Queen on her visits to club regimental dinners.

His Holiness made a short and powerful speech in reply to the toast to his health. He referred to three important links between our two nations—Christian tradition, royal cousinship, and historic military connections, especially the relationship between the Scots Guards and the Preobrazhensky Life Guards. It was therefore appropriate that Captain Andrew Potter[65] flew down from Scotland to pipe in His Holiness, and at the end of the proceedings, to pipe the Ceremony of the Quaich.[66]

---

[65] Royal Scots Dragoon Guards.
[66] Ancient Scottish piping ceremony.

32. With Patriarch Kirill during His Holiness's visit to London in 2016.

It is impossible to underestimate the importance of Orthodoxy in the Russia of today. Whilst in the West, and particularly in Britain, Christianity is on the decline and churches closing in quick succession, the opposite is true in Russia. It seems that the severe persecution of the church in Soviet times has led to an instinctive national Christian renaissance. All over the country, on Sundays and feast days, the bells ring out loudly and confidently. Crowds of people—fathers, mothers, and children—fill the churches, and significantly, I think, eat family lunch together. It reminds me of what England was like not too many years ago, before the decline of church attendance and the breakdown of many families. Under the leadership of Patriarch Kirill, more than eight hundred monasteries have reopened, and many of them are attracting younger postulants.

Thousands of churches have been either restored or rebuilt. For example, over the past few years, over fifty in Moscow alone!

This Orthodox Christian renaissance also impacts behaviour. There is little appetite for identity politics, cancel culture, political correctness, same-sex marriage, LGBTQIA, sex-reassignment surgery, and other manifestations of confused Western philosophy. In Orthodox Russia, men are men, women are women, and morality is fairly clearly defined. Respect for family life, including the elderly and unborn, is noticeable across Russia. Life is precious and should be celebrated, not destroyed.

The final word in this chapter should go to Oliver Clement:[67]

> I liked the union in the orthodox tradition of the sense of mystery and the sense of liberty, the absence of moralising, the simple but profound understanding of salvation as the victory of life, man in the image of the Trinity, the importance given to the Holy Spirit and to beauty and the cosmos, the prayer for universal salvation—and so much more.

---

[67] Oliver Clement, French Orthodox Theologian 1921 - 2009

9

AFTERTHOUGHT

As I write, we are faced with the tragic events in Ukraine. Since 2002, there has been a growing antagonism in the West towards Russia in general and President Putin in particular. This is portrayed in Western media as a politically enlightened West, whose duty is to oppose and contain a dangerous Russia. In my view, however, the issue is far deeper than this.

Nietzsche[68] is popularly attributed with the statement, "The death of God." But in fact, he did not declare the death of God but observed the decline of theistic belief throughout the West. He pointed out that such a decline would seriously alter philosophical perceptions and moral attitudes.

Fortunately, his prognosis went unheard in Russia. Despite the violent political bombardment against religion, and Christianity in particular, Russia kept the faith against all the odds. This is the nature of

---
[68] Frederich Nietzsche 1844 - 1900

'the Russian soul', a term used by Gogol, Tolstoy, and Dostoyevsky in reference to the uniqueness of the Russian national identity.

History bears witness to the Byzantine achievement of which Russia became the spiritual heir, the third Rome. The achievement was the recognition of the indivisible link between church and state, God and man,—the true balance between the spiritual and the physical without which no civilisation can survive. The real polarisation between West and Russia is not just about economics and democracy but about core beliefs.

Western culture is in decline. The economic signs are obvious; the cultural ones are clear. Less obvious to a materially blinded populace is the spiritual vacuum. Western civilization was based on Judaic Christian values. These values have been increasingly replaced by 'woke' influence which is anti traditional family values. This is at the heart of Western decline.

Russia preserves, almost miraculously, the ancient Christian faith. It permeates the very atmosphere, despite the vulgar manifestation of wealth which naturally obsessed the lucky few in the first decade of freedom from communism. That faith lies deep within the soul of every Russian and needs only to be stirred to create a truly Christian nation, whose mission may be vital in the present chaotic Western world.

It takes a good persecution to stimulate faith. Look

at the example of Job. The more he was persecuted, the more he believed, and his faith prevailed.

Thus, a valuable aspect of the communist oppression was the stimulation of Christianity. Even more so the preservation of the ancient Orthodox faith which, cocooned in isolation, was immune from the modernist movement, that has all but destroyed Western Christianity.

Whilst Western Christianity is divided, declining, and immersed in humanism, Russian Orthodoxy is united, strong, and influencing life from the highest to the lowest. Christianity plays a growingly importance in daily life, impacting on morality, culture, and commerce. The church is becoming central whilst in the West, it is increasingly marginalised.

One still hears critics of Russia calling it the Soviet Union, symbolic of the West's inability to distinguish between the Soviet Union and Russia.

The Soviet Union was an aberration in the long course of Russian history. The brutal infliction of atheistic communism on an inherently religious people—the Russian soul. It is essential that the West quickly develops a balanced understanding of Russia, its leaders, and its people. For example, a Western reporter asked many Russians, "Would you not like to have democracy?" to which, "We prefer stability", was the general answer.

Without such an appreciation, polarisation of West

and East will develop to dangerous levels. The West should not just reluctantly accept Russia because of its gas and amazing natural resources. Rather, it should enthusiastically encourage friendship because of the insights and advantages to be gained!

In February 1990, Mikhail Gorbachev and US Secretary of State James Baker met in Moscow. During their discussions, Baker promised that NATO would not expand, "an inch to the East". Other Western leaders took on the promise.

In March 1991, John Major could not foresee, "circumstances now or in the future where East European countries would become members of NATO."

Douglas Hurd stated, "No plans in NATO to include the countries of Eastern and Central Europe in NATO."

Moscow initially trusted these pledges, and so did President Putin—initially. However, with the recent waves of NATO expansion, particularly in 2004 and 2009, the situation is now very different. Russia, with justification, feels threatened.

Russia has a strong economy, and its rich resources include diamonds, coal, timber, cotton, magnesium, gold, silver, and, of course, oil and gas. With the advance of global warming, Russian agriculture, already a significant contributor to GDP, will greatly benefit partly due to its famous black soil. And vineyards now flourish along the shores of the Black Sea. Perhaps the new, independent Britain would do well to put aside its Western prejudice and reach out to Russia as a significant trading partner, thereby appreciating the ancient ties of a thousand years.

Unfortunately the war in Ukraine is really a battle between the American led West and Russia. Ukraine is the battlefield. Kiev can never be divorced from Russia which was born the Kievan Rus. Eventually a diplomatic solution will be found based on a profound understanding of regional history and culture- very difficult for many Western minds to understand. Estonia, though once part of the Russian Empire is very different, partly because of its Germanic Lutheran roots. I don't believe that Russia has any desire to start a conflict there- despite the poor treatment of many ethnic Russians living there. In a hundred years the Estonian Russian population- based on present birth rates- may be in the majority anyway and self determination might prevail! Without international interference the family bonds across the three nations can eventually bring about common sense and peace.

As Sir Winston Churchill was credited with saying "jaw-jaw is better than war-war". May our political elites act accordingly!

CPSIA information can be obtained
at www.ICGtesting.com
Printed in the USA
BVHW081551280223
659388BV00012B/561/J